MIX
Papier aus verantwortungsvollen Quellen
Paper from responsible sources
FSC® C105338
FSC
www.fsc.org

Felix Christoph Lotzin

The Emperor on the Battlefield

Napoleon's Worth as a Military Commander

Anchor Academic
Publishing

Lotzin, Felix Christoph: The Emperor on the Battlefield: Napoleon's Worth as a Military Commander, Hamburg, Diplomica Verlag GmbH 2012

ISBN: 978-3-95489-007-1
Print: Anchor Academic Publishing, an Imprint of Diplomica® Verlag GmbH, Hamburg, 2012

Bibliographical Information of the German National Library:
The German National Library lists this publication in the German National Bibliography. Detailed bibliographic data can be found at: http://dnb.d-nb.de

The digital publication (eBook) of this work with the ISBN 978-3-95489-507-6 can be purchased on the general market or directly from the publisher.

I Table of Contents

II Table of Contents

III Table of Figures

I used to say of him that his presence on the field made the difference of forty thousand men.

Arthur Wellesley, 1. Duke of Wellington

1. Introduction

Though centuries have passed since the rise and fall of Napoleon, his military performance continues to fuel discussion among scholars of history and military science. Scientific discourse about him and the battles and campaigns fought during his age are extensive, nevertheless most research on this topic can broadly be divided into two approaches: historical and from a practical perspective employed by military science. Without conflicting the other, these complement one another, as they independently attempt to explore very different aspects of Napoleonic warfare.

The first approach is the historical perspective, practiced – among many others – by the likes of Blanning[1] or Smith[2]. Scholars focus on the broad lines of the military encounters and the grand strategy[3] as the central theme, interpreted in light of social and cultural aspects as well. A work of such breadth would usually be written by a historian and would be culminating in a good descriptive impression and an overview of most of the aspects of the Napoleonic times. Due to the nature of historical science, empirical data would normally only be used in a qualitative way without employing in-depth quantitative analysis.[4] Moreover the broader perspective is normally emphasized at the expense of

1 Blanning (1996).
2 Smith (2005).
3 In this thesis I will use the definitions of grand strategy, strategy, grand tactics and tactics as proposed by Chandler (2001).
4 E. g. statements along the lines of ‚he fielded more troops' or ‚he had a higher amount of artillery at his disposal'. These statements, although backed by numbers, do not give insight into the size of the effect or the nature of it and therefore can not qualify as quantitative analysis.

detailed aspects and so only statistics of the highest importance are included so not to obscure the leitmotif of history.

Military scientists and practitioners using the second approach usually focus on campaigns and describe the course of them and the important battles that took place during them. Their work is highly detailed and covers many different aspects of Napoleonic warfare. Logistics, infantry tactics, cavalry attacks and artillery bombardments are explained in great detail and their effects are scrutinised. These works usually contain high amounts of empirical data about all the different subjects and facets of contemporary warfare. Nevertheless the focus is on the strategy and the tactics and although numbers are taken into account, their exact impact is not worked out in detail through a quantitative and methodical analysis. Their focus on the military factors furthermore prevents these works to give a comprehensive view of the Napoleonic times but makes them dependent on the general approach discussed before.

Although both approaches can be combined for a very detailed qualitative description of Napoleonic warfare, history and times there is an evident lack of thorough empirical analysis of Napoleons military efficiency. Recent research in economic science has seen an increasing number of papers, books and theories addressing the subject of conflict from an economical and rational choice perspective. Starting with the analysis of 'rent seeking' by Gordon Tullock, several other important theorists[5] have ventured out to study the different aspects of conflict that border both social sciences and economics. This thesis attempts to apply their theories of

[5] I especially owe much to the work of Hirshleifer, who studied conflicts for years and always encouraged other economists to apply the economic theories to other field of scientific work.

conflict to the battles of the Napoleonic age and to test several assumptions derived from the so called Contest Success Functions that have been put forth as models for the prediction of conflict outcomes. Although these concepts have been around for several years and sparked frequent discussion, there are only some works that actually try to verify these theories by applying them on actual data.

Hence this thesis seeks to explore the following two working hypotheses: Firstly, that Napoleon's alleged military superiority in terms of skill and battlefield competence over his peers can be empirically quantified and proven. Secondly, that the results of Napoleonic warfare can be predicted by applying the theory of Contest Success Functions to these battles.[6]

To address these claims this paper is organized into this introduction and four different sections, with eleven chapters in total as follows:

Theory

The first of the conceptual sections summarizes the theoretical underpinning behind the economical understanding of conflict. This so called 'second approach'[7]

---

[6] Interestingly, a similar approach was chosen by two research teams before. In 1962 the Research Analysis Corporation conducted a study on the Lancaster Equations for the United States Department of Defence. [The Lancaster Equations being early developments of Contest Success Functions there are some similarities in the approach, especially in the use of regressions. Willard concluded that the Lancaster Equations only had a poor predictive value for his data. Compare Willard (1962) for further information.
The second research work is the so-called Quantitative Judgment Method Analysis developed by Colonel Dupuy. [Dupuy(1985)] This analysis started from a historical perspective by manually fitting curves until the conduct of a battle could be predicted. Although this method has high value for predicting the outcome of battles, this is only accomplished by using dozens of variables to increase the predictive value. Although some of the curves are variants of the Logit-Function this thesis relies on as well, the method used and the sheer magnitude of explaining variables makes comparison only possible for small aspects.

[7] Hirshleifer (1994).

and its merits are outlined and the history of these theoretical concepts is explained. Chapter three introduces the Ratio Contest Success Function (RCSF) put forth by Tullock and the Difference Contest Success Function (DCSF) employed by Hirshleifer, the concepts for predicting probabilities of success in conflict theory.

History

The fourth and fifth chapters are used to outline the actual conditions during the Napoleonic wars and the data used for this study. The focus of this part is especially what we actually do now about these battles and how it may be used. The fourth chapter gives a brief report on warfare during the Napoleonic ages. A special emphasis lies on an analysis that evaluates if the key parameters have been homogenous over the time and what kind of technology was employed during these battles. The results are then compared with the demands of conflict theory. The fifth chapter then explicates the data set. The different variables that could be obtained are introduced and at last the scope of the further analysis is specified. This is done by picking the variables that actually can be used for an in-depth quantitative.

Modelling

The third part of the thesis is of especial importance, as the focus of this work is to answer the two hypotheses by empirical work. In the four chapters that deal with the actual modelling, the theory is applied on the historical data to yield the results we need to verify the working hypotheses. After the two different estimators used have been introduced in chapter six, the chapters seven and eight deal with utilising each of the estimators to answer these questions. The results from the estimates are interpreted and are compared in chapter nine. In addition, chapter nine attempts to weigh the explanatory value of the two approaches and places them in the historical perspective.

Résumé The last section of my thesis contains two chapters. Chapter ten answers comments on Napoleon's personal worth on the battlefield and applies the findings of the empirical work on three short case studies.[8] The subsequent summary then merges the results of the whole study and concludes with follow-up questions for future research.

---

[8] The case studies then should answer if Napoleon really had the impact of 40,000 soldiers, like Wellington attributed it to him.

I Theory

There are but two powers in the world, the sword and the mind. In the long run the sword is always beaten by the mind.

Napoleon Bonaparate

2. The Economy of Conflict – The Second Approach

To understand how economist approach conflict, we first have to master one very important concept of modern economics, that forms the centre of economic science as we do know it. This is the fictive *homo oeconomicus*. This conceptual person takes everything into account and then tries to maximise its utility[9] by deciding what to do. Possibilities can include such trivial decision like the one between going to work or staying at home[10] or between buying a car or saving the money. In the later case the *homo oeconomicus* would buy a car if he values owning and using it more than the money he has to pay for it. We always assume that this individual would make a rational choice, based on its assumptions about the different possibilities. Conventional economics do know only one method for this person to make a living: producing useful goods or services and trade.[11] Although this constitutes by far the biggest part of economic transactions it nevertheless does not catch these in total and omits the other side of human nature and behaviour.

Interestingly, this strict focus on producing goods evolved only over time. The works that founded economic science did refer quite often to a very different aspect of economic behaviour:

> *"The efforts of men are utilized in two different ways: they are directed to the production or transformation of economic goods,* ***or else to the appropriation of goods produced by others.****"* – Vilfredo Pareto

---

9 The concept of utility will not be detailed here, as it is common economic knowledge. For our uses it should be sufficient to understand utility as the amount one does value a specific situation.

10 But even these decisions can be quite hard when the structural conditions are a bit more complicated – e. g. when welfare could be paid out.

11 Compare the definition of economics of most standard textbooks, e. g. Marshall (1977).

Adam Smith[12] and Vilfredo Pareto both made many references to conflicts and how these shaped human interactions and especially decisions. The merit for reintroducing this dualism to economic acting goes to Thomas Schelling, who in his book *The Strategy of Conflict*[13] outlined many concepts[14] that nowadays are part of the standard economic curriculum, after they for some time had been of no importance[15]. Especially the game theory[16] profited from his works, which mainly deal with the underlying concepts of behaviour. Several later scientists then started to sketch out a theory of conflict interactions. During the 1970es Tullock[17] "was [...] the first to employ standard analytical building blocks [...] for dealing with conflict interactions".[18] By this inventive and new approach it was for the first time possible to conduct a thorough analysis of conflicts from an economic perspective and to foster a better understanding of how conflicts actually do work.

But conflict theory is not so very one sided to explain only how conflict evolves – it even does not predict that all the time clashes have to occur. Nash-equilibriums not only include the best amount of input for a conflict, but can explain cooperation as well. To show how the parts of conflict theory interact, we have to distinguish four aspects that together explain what happens before, during and after:[19]

---

12 Adam Smiths „The Wealth of Nations" cites war and conflict regularly.

13 Schelling (1960).

14 The most widely known of these is the concept of *commitment*, where one side constrains the options of its adversary by binding itself.

15 Nevertheless these mostly ‚conflict-less' times saw the development of the Lancaster Laws, which were early special cases of the Ratio Contest Success Function which will be discussed later.

16 The game theory attempts to capture behaviour in strategic situations by mathematical terms.

17 Tullock (1974).

18 Hirshleifer (2001), p. 4.

19 These four aspects are presented in Hirshleifer (2001), p. 13.

Sources of Conflict

These can range from different preference sets up to totally irrational reasons for conflicts, e.g. hate, distrust or love. They are the starting point for the whole affair. Depending on their shapes they can make conflicts more intense or make it easy to bridge the gap and cooperate.[20] Because this thesis analyses the battles and their outcomes, the sources of conflict during the Napoleonic ages are not to be discussed here in depth. Suffice to say that there are several brilliant books written by historians that cover these conflicts and how they evolved.[21] For our analysis it is only necessary to assume that there is conflict and that during the battles it can not be solved by any kind of cooperation or agreement short of a surrender, so that the battles have to be fought out.

Technology of Conflict

This category includes the analysis of the technology actually used to fight out the conflict – either in a metaphorical way where leaflets or television campaigns could be the technology, or when these measures are actually used to have fights and wars. The importance of the tools used to wage a conflict lies within the differences of them. Without distinguishing between them, a rational choice is not possible. Therefore it is not only necessary to differentiate among these instruments, but for every choice it has to be considered how to get this kind of technology, how to use it, what the costs are and what the impact upon the conflict will be.

---

20 Amazingly it can even happen, that intense sources of conflict can ease cooperation, e. g. when both parties involved are willing to give everything up for the fight and both parties know this and do not want to take the chance.

21 Although all the books in the references should be able to shed some light on the sources of the Napoleonic wars, especially „The Napoleonic Wars: Rise and Fall of an Empire“ by Barnes and Fisher (2004) gives a good first impression of them.

In contrast to conflicts with diverging sources, it is not always possible to compare conflicts them when the technologies are not the same among them. Each set of technology offers a unique set of choices and possibilities to the actors. Hence different conflicts can only be compared if some of consistency holds true for the situations that are to be analysed. It will be of importance to have a closer look at the technology used during the Napoleonic wars to make sure that the battles can be compared without blurring the results.

Modelling of Conflict

The actual modelling of the conflict tries to put the interactions during it into a theory, which most of the time is expressed at least partially through mathematics. This is generally a problem of "optimization on the decision-making level",[22] where we are interested in how probable it is to win a certain conflict or how big a share of the booty we can expect.

During the modelling several aspects have to be taken into account. Technology, resources, the intensity of the conflict – all these are variables that might influence the result and therefore have to be checked for their impact. There are umpteen different approaches to actually modelling a conflict, from black-box-models, where no assumptions are made about what actually happens, to the highly complex war games of the military, where thousands of variables are taken into account. Small level, multi party conflicts with homogenous technologies among the parties are of a special interest. These approaches include the Contest Success Functions (CSF), which model the probability of winning a certain contest or conflict subject to the inputs by the parties involved and which shall be used later on.

[22] See Hirshleifer(2001), p. 18.

Consequences of Conflict

Consequences can range from getting no or less money to very grave ones like getting killed or defeated in a military struggle – even cooperation and peace are possible. Military battles often not only yielded partial results in the style of a won battle, but could lead to crushing defeats of whole countries. These consequences have to be taken into account when the actual modelling takes place, although some interesting results can be obtained about them during modelling as well.

It would be beyond the scope of this work to include all the different consequences into the analysis of the battles. For this thesis the consequences of a certain battle are either to hold one's ground or the retreat from the battlefield and hence the loss of terrain, initiative and cohesion among the forces.

Conclusion

But in how far is this of reference for the two working hypotheses? The first hypothesis states, that the presence of Napoleon had an impact on the French probability of winning a battle. This is actually both an amendment to the technology of conflict and the modelling. By making the presence of Napoleon possible, the technology set is augmented with one more option and this addition has to be integrated into the modelling as well.

The second hypothesis postulates that the battles of that era can be modelled via the Contest Success Functions. These, like we shall see in the next chapter, say that the input of the competitors – the committed forces in military terms – can be used to predict the outcome of such a conflict situation. Therefore this hypothesis augments the technology set as well by introducing the input of forces and makes a statement about the kind of modelling actually to be used.

The most important aspects of conflict for testing these hypotheses therefore are the actual modelling of the conflict and – to a much smaller degree – the technology of the conflict.

3. Modelling Contest via the Contest Success Functions

It is important to understand some basic concepts about Contest Success Functions in general before moving on to the special Contest Success Functions by Tullock and Hirshleifer. Hence this chapter will first introduce basic aspects of Contest Success Functions, before the two special ones are introduced and analysed. At last it will be discussed when which function might be applicable.

a. *Contest Success Functions in General*

The concept of economic contest evolved, when Tullock introduced a new approach to measuring the welfare costs of monopolies.[23] In his paper he argued that the traditional approach to calculate the costs of a monopoly for society were flawed, because they omitted the costs that are connected with the struggle about the monopoly. In principle the patrons are overreached in a monopoly case, as the producer can charge them prices that are higher then they would be in the case of competition. Therefore the monopolist can make a higher profit then he could have by selling the same amount on a competitive market – which is highly desirable for him.

Additionally to these burden to the consumers, there is another burden to society: the costs of the struggle for this desirable case of being the monopolist. These costs can be varied and can include lobbying costs, marketing, new facilities or even bribes - to name only a few. Tullock showed that these costs also have to be taken into account when calculating the costs a monopoly had for society. Starting with this problem of the so-called 'rent-seeking'[24], many more conflicts were recognised.

[23] Tullock (1967).
[24] This term was actually coined by Krueger (1974).

Hirshleifer then put forth the argumentation that these thoughts should be broadened and that the models that had been designed to describe rent-seeking compromised only a small part of a much bigger family of Contest Success Functions. He argued that these Contest Success Functions could be applied to every conflict situation to provide it with a theoretical background. Furthermore his impression was, that on the border of social sciences and economics these Contest Success Functions would offer new opportunities to shed light on how conflicts evolve and especially on who will be the winning party.[25] During further research it emerged, that there are some characteristics that all Contest Success Functions have to share and which can be stated with an axiomatic character.[26]

As these are best expressed in mathematical terms, we first need to define the variables we are going to use:

let	n	be the finite number of contestants in this contest;
let	c_i	be the amount of effort the ith contestant puts into winning this conflict measured in cost units;
let	$p_i(c_i)$	be the probability of the ith contestant to emerge as the winner of this conflict.

Then we can express the three absolutely needed axioms about Contest Success Functions this way:

---

25 Compare Hirshleifer (1989) for more information.

26 For a formal analysis check Skaperdas (1994). For the sake of simplicity only the three most important axioms will be discussed here. It will become evident, that only these will be needed to create econometric models by which to estimate the exact CSF later.

A1. $\sum_{i=1}^{n} p_i(c_i) = 1$

and $p_i(c_i) \geq 0$ for all i

and $p_i(c_i) > 0$ if $c_i > 0$.

A2. $\frac{\Delta p_i(c_i)}{\Delta c_i} \geq 0$ for all i

and $\frac{\Delta p_i(c_i)}{\Delta c_j} \leq 0$ for all $j \neq i$.

A3. For any permutation π of the n contestants $p_{\pi(i)}(c) = p(c_{\pi_1}) = p(c_{\pi 2}) = \ldots = p(c_{\pi_n})$ will hold true.[27]

Axiom 1 states that all the probabilities sum up to one in the end, the probability of winning of every contestant is at least zero and that if you put any kind of effort into the contest, your probability of succeeding will not be zero. Axiom 2 dilates this with the presumption that if you put more effort into the contest your probability of succeeding will rise and that it will fall if any other contestants decides to invest more. The anonymity property statement of Axiom 3 then predicates, that the probability of winning for every contestant does only rely on his effort, not on who he his.

Any kind of function that tries to model contest has to fulfil these requirements to give predictions that are at least conceivable. Nevertheless, these axioms are only the lowest bar every kind of economic modelling has to take. In no way do they differentiate good models from bad ones - but only models that could describe reality from those models that never could do so. During research two families of Contest Success Functions evolved, which dominate conflict economics

[27] This approach owes greatly to Skaperdas (1994), who was among the first to point out these fundamentals in such a clear manner.

nowadays. Both have unique features and fulfil all the three axioms introduced above, so that they can be used for modelling. Named after their most striking characteristics these are the Ratio Contest Success Function and the Difference Contest Success Function, which will be discussed and explained now.

b. The Ratio Contest Success Function

In Tullock's basic model of 'rent-seeking' the probability of winning for a contestant[28] was determined by the ratio of the own effort and all efforts together. For the case of only two players this can be expressed as:

$$p_1 = \frac{c_1}{c_1 + c_2}.$$

This fairly basic model was in turn amended by several papers[29] and evolved by adding a factor m, the so called 'mass-effect-parameter', and a factor k_i which measures how efficient the effort of the ith player is.[30] The amended and generalized Tullock function then evolves into the generally applicable Ratio Contest Success Function:

$$p_i = \frac{(k_i c_i)^m}{\sum_{j=1}^{n} (k_j c_j)^m}.$$

The Ratio Contest Success Function obviously fulfils all the three axioms we established during the general approach to Contest Success Functions and therefore does not conflict with reality per se.[31] Furthermore, it has a special attribute that characterises it: $p_i(\lambda c_i) = p_i(c_i)$ for all i. This implies that

[28] Contestant and player will from now on be used as synonyms.

[29] Hirshleifer (1994) credits among others Hillmann and Katz (1984), Corcoran and Karels (1985) and Hillmann and Samet (1987) with the improvement of the Tullock model.

[30] This factor k_i can be the same for all players – a special case when it looses it meaning – but we can not assume this without proof.

[31] Proof for this is trivial and can be found in Skaperdas (1994).

if all the inputs are multiplied by a fixed amount λ, no results and probabilities will change.[32] Using the Ratio Contest Success Function the probability of winning a conflict does only depend on the ratio of the efforts involved, the 'mass-effect-parameter' (m) and the efficiency of the individual players (k_i). If all players increase their efforts with the same ratio, no effects will occur. The contrary happens when the players increase their efforts by the same amount – the probabilities will change then.[33]

Interestingly the behaviour of the Ratio Contest Success Function depends only on the 'mass-effect-parameter' m when only one player changes his efforts. Regardless of the level of m it always holds true that $p_i = p_j$ if $k_i c_i = k_j c_j$. For $m \leq 1$ the player will face diminishing returns to his efforts all the time. When $m > 1$ increasing returns to effort are possible at the start, with diminishing returns later on. This is illustrated by Figure 1.

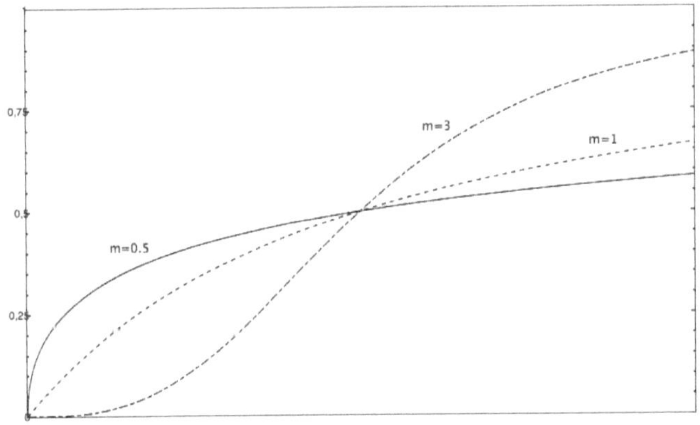

Figure 1. Ratio Contest Success Function

32 Proof:
$$\frac{(\lambda k_i c_i)^m}{\sum_{j=1}^{n}(\lambda k_j c_j)^m} = \frac{\lambda^m (k_i c_i)^m}{\lambda^m \sum_{j=1}^{n}(k_j c_j)^m} = \frac{\lambda^m}{\lambda^m} \cdot \frac{(k_i c_i)^m}{\sum_{j=1}^{n}(k_j c_j)^m} = \frac{(k_i c_i)^m}{\sum_{j=1}^{n}(k_j c_j)^m} = p_i(c_i).$$

33 Except for the special case when all the players invest the same effort and are equally effective in applying it.

c. *The Difference Contest Success Function*

Although Tullock's model obviously has its merits – for instance it is easy to understand and work with - there are nevertheless several flaws that can render it less usable for some applications. Hirshleifer criticises, that "there is an enormous gain when your side's forces increase from just a little smaller than the enemy's to just a little larger".[34] Especially when the efforts of both sides are high the Ratio Contest Success Function will not award further input with a considerable increase in the probability of winning[35] but does predict only a very small effect on the probabilities. Instead of amending the Ratio Contest Success Function to compensate for these flaws, he proposed another sort of model that is based not on the ratio of the efforts but on the differences between them.[36]

Keeping in mind the axioms A1 to A3 and further postulating that success in contest depends upon the difference between the resources committed, he offered the following model, which is now known as the Difference Contest Success Function:

$$p_1 = \frac{1}{1+e^{\gamma(c_2-c_1)}}.$$

This formula is a specific case of the family of the logistic functions, where γ is the 'mass-effect-parameter' for the difference form. This family of functions has several special features that make them very attractive for describing probabilities. The most important of these attributes in the case of the Difference Contest Success Function is the returned

34 Hirshleifer (1994), p. 93.
35 This is because of the diminishing returns to effort.
36 It can be argued that amending the Ratio Contest Success Function would not have been possible at all.

value, which always is between 0 and 1. Similarly to the case of the Ratio Contest Success Function, this simple case with two contestants can be generalized by introducing an efficiency parameter k_i for the individual players and by raising the amount from 2 to n. The result is the general form of the Difference Contest Success Function:

$$p_i = \frac{e^{\gamma \cdot k_i \cdot c_i}}{\sum_{j=1}^{n} e^{\gamma \cdot k_j \cdot c_j}}.^{37}$$

Where the Ratio Contest Success Function was not affected by proportional increases of all efforts, the Difference Contest Success Function is not affected when all players increase their efforts by the same absolute amount.[38] Contrary to the Ratio Contest Success Function, in this case the 'mass-effect-parameter' γ does not change the general shape of the returns to efforts curve but does influence how steep these effects are.

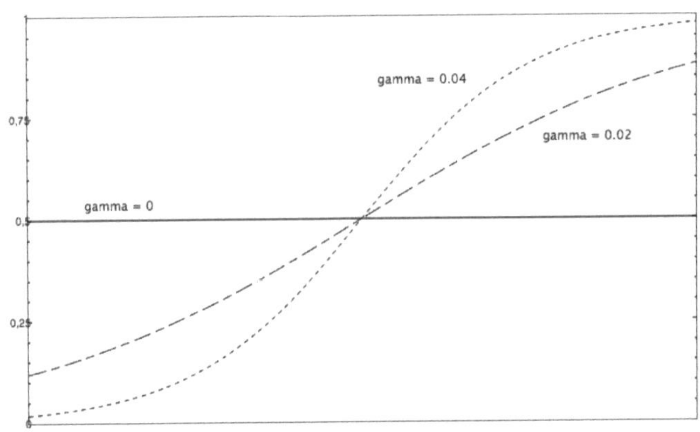

Figure 2. Difference Contest Success Function

[37] The proof that the Ratio Contest Success Function does comply with A1 to A3 is trivial. See Skaperdas (1994) for further information.

[38] Mathematically this can be expressed as $p(c+\lambda) = p(c)$, where λ is a vector of the same dimension as c and $\lambda_i = \lambda_j$ holds true for all i,j.

A visual comparison of the two Contest Success Functions shows us, that under some circumstances both can look remarkably alike. This is the case when the players commit nearly the same amount of effort. For every Ratio CSF there exists then a Difference CSF that has exactly the same increase in probability for a further unit of effort. [39]

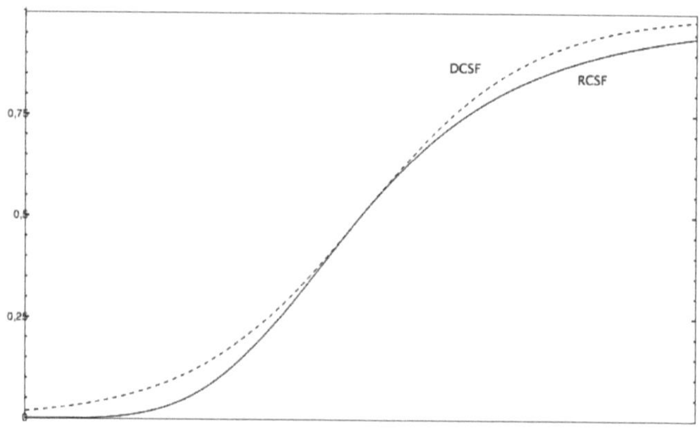

Figure 3. DCSF ($\gamma = 0.04$) and RCSF ($m = 4$)

Hence it can be complicated to differentiate between the two kinds of Contest Success Functions practically, especially when the measured efforts of the contestants do not vary much among each other and among the contests. In cases where either the efforts among the contestants or among the contests do vary more it gets easier to differentiate and to decide upon the function with the greater explanatory value.

Theoretically we would expect the RCSF to be of higher value if the contest is conducted under optimal circumstances – where total information for all the players and perfect

[39] To get the same slope in this point $\gamma = \frac{m}{c}$ has to be fulfilled. For proof of this skip to Appendix A.

homogeneity of the efforts can be assumed, the RCSF is normally chosen. When we expect frictions to happen and decisions problems for the players to arise, we would assume that the DCSF would prevail.

This is a result of the way the functions are modelled and is much easier to understand, if one assumes the analogy of a battlefield. The RCSF would describe the battle pretty accurately if the battlefield were flat, had no fog, offered no places to hide and we could use all our units simultaneously and wherever we wanted them to be right at this moment. We then would expect the larger force to use its superior numbers for a concentrated assault. It would be logical for the defending force to concentrate as well, as smaller units would have even smaller chances of winning. Therefore we expect an all-out battle of attrition that concentrates in one spot with all the forces.

The DCSF describes a totally different battlefield, on which movement, dispersion and knowledge about the enemy are all limited. We then can interpret the difference between the two parties involved as reserves that the superior force still can use, after the whole enemy force has been engaged. This force then could be used to fight only at certain spots and not against all of the enemy force. Hence we expect this kind of battle to be divided into smaller encounters where different units fight each other, with one side having reserves in the backhand. This model hence should provide to be a better fit if we try to analyse battles that only lasted a certain time and so could not evolve into battles of attrition.

II History

History is the version of past events that people have decided to agree upon.

Napoleon Bonaparate

4. The Essentials about Napoleonic Warfare

During the discussion of economic conflict theory it emerged, that there are four aspects to every analysis of conflict on which light has to be shed. We established before, that the sources of conflict and the consequences do not belong to the topics of this thesis. In the last chapter we examined a way of modelling the conflict via the Contest Success Functions. Nevertheless there still does remain the question of the technology of conflict. Necessarily this question could not be answered in an abstract way, as everything can belong to it. We therefore need to discuss it directly along the lines of the conflict explored. The following chapter is based upon several historical works that are listed in the references in detail. Two of these were of special importance: *The Art of Warfare on Land* by David Chandler[40] and *Tactics and the Experience of Battle in the Age of Napoleon* by Rory Muir[41].

As a battle only forms a small cut-out of a war, war itself constitutes only one way of conflict. During a war everything can be an instrument to be turned against the enemy – together they make the technology of this war. From the more subtle ones to the brutish attacks all have to be taken into account, when deciding what constitutes the technology. Recurring on the working hypotheses, we do not need to deal with the technology of these wars in total, but only with what could be applied during the battles that formed the culminations of warfare in these times. We now will have to examine the technology of Napoleonic era battles and will start with the armament of these times. The soldiers that could be fielded, the organisation of the armies and their tactics are examined afterwards.

---

40 Chandler (2001).

41 Muir (1998).

Armament

Although Napoleon is known to be one of the greatest generals of all time, he never was very interested in new technologies and how these could be applied to warfare.[42] Since the times of Frederick the Great only small inventions had been made and generally the armies were still equipped with the same weapons.

The *infantry* was armed with muskets and, in the case of the light battalions, with rifled guns. Special importance was laid upon the use of the bayonet, as the firearms were still clumsy and took long times to reload. *Cavalry* was equipped with sabres and pistols, the heavy ones[43] still wearing armour and the light cavalry only protected by the normal uniform. Only the *artillery* equipment had changed noteworthy after lighter guns, the so-called field guns, had been introduced into service. The Royal French Army had been the first to utilize these advanced guns and soon the other countries had to improve as well. Nevertheless no big inventions were made during the Napoleonic era that had a notable impact on the armament of the troops fielded. Hence armament can be treated as having been homogenous in nature.[44]

Soldiers

Although the concept of conscription can be traced back to the Fyrd of Anglo-Saxon-England or even to the Ilkum of the Babylonian Empire, for some decades the armies had only

---

[42] Chandler (2001) argues that he even disbanded the experimental balloon companies.

[43] The cuirassiers.

[44] It is important to differentiate between the arms in general having been homogenous and all units being homogenously armed. The former was the case, as every country knew about guns, sabres and rifles. The latter we can not assume, as the countries armed their troops differently.

consisted of professional soldiers. The military profession was often regarded to be one of the lowest forms of employment to choose, so that many soldiers had been forced into the ranks or were former convicts. This dramatically changed in France after the revolution had forced many officers of the Royal French Army – most of them from the nobility – to flee the country. The new armies were drawn from among the population by the system called 'levée en masse', the first conscription of modern times. Soldiers recruited by these means had a higher motivation and were noted for their patriotic attitude. As the other countries were forced to field bigger armies as well to cope with this situation, they adopted similar measures.[45] As we will see in the discussion of tactics, this even entailed adopting new approaches to attack, as the new soldiers did not have the same military training the professionals fielded before had had. Anyhow the new tactics could be employed with the old troops as well, so that for the sake of this analysis only the numbers did differ. Hence we will not control for a difference between conscripts and regulars.

Organisation

When Napoleon took over command of the whole French Revolutionary Army, the biggest organisational changes already had been implemented. By then Lazare Carnot, whom revolutionary France mandated with reorganising the armed forces, had already introduced the system of mixed divisions that were made up of infantry, cavalry and artillery and that were complete fighting units in themselves. Napoleon himself made changes to the staff system[46] and introduced the army corps for the first time. The changes by Carnot and himself enabled him to use new approaches to strategy but did not change what actually

[45] Chandler (2001), p. 149.

[46] He clarified the mission of the general staff and was the first to introduce smaller staffs at divisional and corps level. See Chandler (2001).

happened on the battlefield when opposing forces had met. Thus these organisational changes need not to be taken account when conducting predictions for battles at the tactical level.

Tactics

As we have seen, 'Napoleon was no great innovator as a soldier; rather, his genius lay in the practical field.'[47] He employed many new tactics and invented innovative ways of doing combat. There are two tactical manoeuvres that are most striking when Napoleon's battles are scrutinized.

Firstly, he often seized a *central position* and forced the enemy to divide into two parts, breaking up the fight into small battles against numerically inferior foes while pinning down the bigger part of the enemy with a small part of his own forces. After winning the first engagement he then would proceed to attack the main force, employing flanking attacks and massed numbers. His second stratagem was the *envelopment*, used against numerically inferior adversaries. He diverted attraction from his main force by employing a part of his army as a blocking force and then outflanked the enemy, thrusting into his flanks.

Although these two strategies seem to be pretty obvious, they were not in these times, because most of the generals that were Napoleon's peers still adhered to the believe in a rigid system of giving battle, manoeuvres without fighting and embanked wars. Thence we have to take the difference between Napoleon and his adversaries into account, at least until they were able to acquire and emulate these tactics as well.

---

[47] Chandler (2001), p. 151.

Conclusion

We can regard the technology vector we need for our further studies as consisting of two elements: The number of the forces involved and Napoleon's presence. Argumentation that checking for Napoleon's presence is necessary is pretty straightforward, he employed new tactics and strategies and other generals tried to emulate him. Therefore it is of interest to know how much the outcomes of the battles would be affected by him. If this would not have been the case, then his new approaches would have been useless and no one would have felt the need to emulate him.

As we have seen above, the armament of the forces and their organisation in divisions[48] were much alike among the warring factions, so that we can assume homogenous elements of effort. These elements can then be linked to the size of the force present at the battle, so that we can summarize the effort of the contestants as being the soldiers fighting. Hence the force size is the second component of the technology vector we can use to explain these battles.

[48] This is the main manoeuvre element on the battlefield, as a mixed division is capable of fighting on its own.

5. The Data Set

Without reliable data a quantitative approach to battles necessarily would have to fail. It is therefore of the utmost importance to gather not only data that provides in-depth information about the conflicts analysed, but also a large enough amount of facts about different battles, so that empirical tools can be applied with reasonable accuracy and significance.[49] This is why collecting the data is very time intensive – except when the data already has been gathered and prepared.

Although it would have been possible to extract the information needed from varying sources of historical work, this would have been very labour intensive and troublesome. Judging the different sources, weighting their reliability and trying to establish correct numbers for a data set large enough to be used during econometric analysis would require extensive historical insight. This would be beyond the scope of a diploma thesis in economics. Nevertheless there exist some books of scientists who gathered extensive information from primary sources and summed them up in accessible volumes.

The source for the data is an extensive volume prepared by Digby Smith[50], the 'Napoleonic Wars Data Book', which lists roughly 2,000 battles and clashes that happened from 1792 to 1815. The data set prepared for this study is accessible in Appendix B and includes the fights that are listed as battles according to general agreement among historic scholars.[51] As not all the observations can be explained individually, this

---

[49] Empirical science and especially econometric tools should only be applied if the data set is of reasonable size, mostly said to be at 50 or more observations.

[50] Smith (1998).

[51] This restriction was chosen because clashes do lack homogeneities, so that comparing them is not possible without analysing each clash on its own. Battles, to the contrary, could only occur if both sides decided to fight or if one opponent was trapped and regularly gave both commanding officers the chance to conduct some kind of planning beforehand.

chapter will give some insight into what the extracted variables describe and why they have been included.

The variable *AC* is an alphanumerical code, describing the region or country the battle was fought in. An extensive list is included in Appendix B if the reader is interested in the actual values. Although knowing where the battle was fought is of no value beforehand it could be used as an explaining variable and substitute for the knowledge about the terrain during the actual empirical research.[52]

The time is encoded afterwards in itemised format with *Day, Month* and *Year* being separate variables. The last chapter emphasized that there could be a link between the military performance of Napoleon and the time. His opponents acquiring skills he in the beginning possessed alone could mean that his performance decreased over time, hence including the time could prove useful for further research on this topic.

Nap is a binary variable that is coded as 1 when Napoleon was the commander in chief of the French Army and 0, if another general was in command. This variable is obviously needed to study the efficiency of Napoleon's military command.

As all the battles where the French were not part of the fighting have been omitted from the data, the variable *Fr* is always encoded as 1.

ForFr and *LosFr* are the French forces engaged and lost during the battle. To make comparisons possible only the

[52] This actually proved to have no positive impact on the predictive value of the models.

forces that actually fought during the battle or were held as a reserve on the battlefield were included, omitting forces that did not see the battlefield. Furthermore when calculating the losses it was important to include always the same categories. Military losses are categorized into Killed in Action (KIA), Missing in Action (MIA), Wounded in Action (WIA) and deserters. As sometimes only the whole sum of all the categories was known they have been included into every calculation, so that different battles can be compared.

At last *VFr* is a binary variable also, which turns 1 at a French victory at the particular battle and 0 if the coalition won. In the rare cases where the outcome was indecisive, both victory variables have been encoded as 1.

The variables for the coalition forces had to be gathered using the same premises and therefore are completely comparable with the French ones, except for minor differences. *Br, Pr, Aus, Rus, SP* and *UN* are binaries which encode the presence of the following nations on the battlefield: Great Britain, Prussia, Austria, Russia, Spain & Portugal and lastly the unnamed smaller countries that sent forces as well.

In cases where coalition armies fought *ForCo* gives the sum of all the contingents present, as mostly it would not have been possible to allocate mixed units with certainty. The variable *LosCo* is the sum of the coalition losses, which have been calculated along the same lines as the French losses and finally *VCo* encodes if the coalition triumphed or lost.

As we have seen, all the variables have been gathered with homogeneity among the different battles in mind. By using the same rules for the forces of France and its enemies, the resulting data may be used to obtain empirical results.

Nevertheless, there are some technical issues that have to be addressed:

1. To answer questions about the winning possibility of certain players we need two types of observations. On the one hand we do need plenty of observations that show the player winning the contest. Some observations are needed on the other hand where the contest is lost. If this were not the case, the model would systematically under- or overestimate the influence of some of the players.

2. Secondly, to estimate the influence of Napoleon, observations are needed with and without him present. Else we could not differentiate between the influence of Napoleon on the French soldiers and their inherent skill.

3. Last but not least: without variation in the force levels running regressions will yield no interpretable results if the models depend on the forces as explanatory variables.

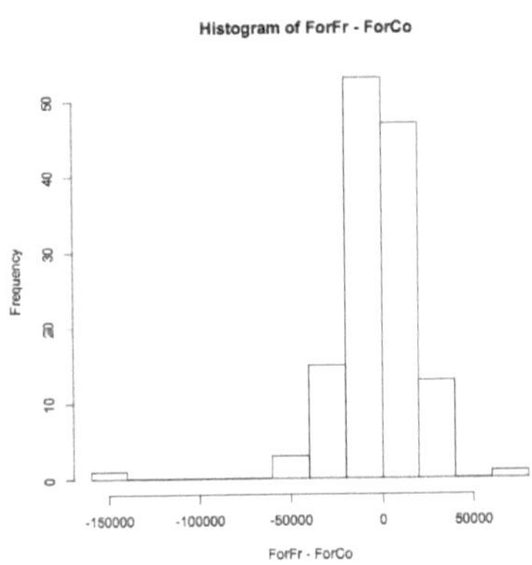

Figure 4. Frequency of French forces less Coalition forces

Checking the data set tells us, if it can keep up with these requirements. Counting the French victories among our battles leaves us with 67 of them and 66 occasions where the French had to leave the field of war as the looser. So the first issue should pose no problem to research where the French are concerned.[53] The second requirement is met by the data set as well. There are 101 battles without and 32 with Napoleon present. Furthermore, in both sub sets are victories and losses alike, so that we do not have to fear constant over- or underestimation. Lastly, variation in the force sizes poses no problems, as they – and especially the difference between them – fluctuate quite much, which is illustrated by Figure 4.

[53] We only do have two observations for the British forces loosing a battle, so the results for them should be scrutinized after running the regression.

III Modelling

A smart model is a good model.

Tyra Banks about handsome models

6. The Two Ways of Estimating a CSF

In the course of this chapter two different approaches to regression analysis will be sketched out, so that it becomes clear how these work generally and when they might be applicable. Both the 'method of least squares' and the 'maximum likelihood method' are very shortly explained and some attention will be paid to the question where and what kind of problems can appear. A detailed introduction into regression analysis can be found in Woolridge (2003) and Tutz (2000) and is not the aim of this work.

a. *The OLS Estimator and its Shortcomings*

The easiest and most common approach of economists to regression analysis is by using the 'Ordinary Least Squares Method' (OSLM). This method changes the parameters until the sum of squared residuals has reached the lowest value possible.[54] The explanatory variables are then linked via a linear transformation[55] to the explained variable. The simplest form of this is the 'two-variable linear regression model', which links only one explanatory variable to an explained one.

$$y = \beta_0 + \beta_1 x + u$$

In this case x is the explaining variable and y the explained one, while u are the unobserved objects we do not want to model or are not able to measure. The functional relationship between x and y is very easy to understand:

y increases by β_1 for every x and

β_0, the intercept, is the value for $x = 0$.

[54] A residual is the difference between an observed value and the value provided by the model.

[55] Essentially the explanatory variable is multiplied by the parameter fitted to it by the model – the so-called coefficient.

The linearity of the model implies, that a one-unit change in x always has the same effects on y, regardless of how big x is in the beginning.[56] This model then can be expanded to include many more variables, but the essentials stay the same: β_i is the increase in y for one more x_i.[57]

Although the necessity of linearity in the parameters might seem to be very restrictive at first, this is not the case. It is easily possible to model quadratic or logarithmic functions – even mixes can be realised. The linearity is only strictly needed for the parameters the model tries to fit, nevertheless the functions can be integrated into the variables, as these can take every value wanted. Hence it poses no problem to model a Ratio CSF via the OSLM, as long as the force ratios and not the forces are treated as independent variables.

OSLM nevertheless has its shortcomings. For a model to be good we would want it to give us unbiased predictions[58] and to predict results that fluctuate only weakly around the real values. Gauß and Markov discovered that the OSLM does fulfil these requirements[59] if some demands can be met – the so-called 'Gauß-Markov-Theorem'.[60] But especially when dichotomy of the explained variable occurs several problems arise, that can belittle the results obtained by using the OLSM.[61]

---

56 All these statements are made for the case that all other things be held equal and u is not present.

57 The model would then be amended to take several explanatory variables into account: $y = \beta_0 + \sum \beta_i x_i + u$.

58 In statistics unbiased means, that the result returned by the model is not generally too high or too low but that the results will over- and underestimate evenly.

59 The OLSM is then the 'Best Linear Unbiased Estimator', the BLUE.

60 For an in-depth discussion of the theorem, the OLSM in general and the BLUE see Wooldridge (2003).

61 The application on binary response variables is called the Linear Probabilistic Model. Regardless of the name it still retains all the attributes of the OLSM.

Firstly, for the OLSM to fulfil these requirements the residuals have to be independent of the values of the explaining variables. With dichotomy this simply is not possible, as the residuals for extreme values are necessarily smaller and thus depend on the values of the explanatory variables.[62] Secondly, these residuals are not normally distributed. Only two residuals can occur for any given x_i, but with only two possible residuals no normal distribution can be even thought of. This implies that when we try to apply the model to a Contest Success Function, the OLSM will not necessarily produce good or even unbiased results.[63]

Notwithstanding these problems, the OLSM can be used to test the applicability of the Ratio CSF on certain contest situations. The easy adaptability of the method and the possibility to include the ratio function as well as multiple further variables makes it a good starting point for research on the Contest Success Functions. However we do have to be aware of the problems that can arise.

b. The Logit-Model

The second method employed in this thesis is the regression analysis via the Logit-Model, a model that is especially useful when the explained variable is categorical in nature, so that dichotomy applies. Whereas fitting the data via the OLSM can give predictive values above one or less than zero, this is impossible to happen with this way of conducting regression analysis. The model fits the data to a curve specified by the family of the logistical equations – hence the Logit-Model.

---

[62] Compare Wooldridge (2003).

[63] It still could produce good results, but rather as a matter of chance.

To understand all the implications of this particular model it is necessary to recreate how it is constructed. Though the model does give predictions about probabilities, it does not work directly with these but with odds. Odds are near siblings of probabilities, as their definition does show:

$$o_i = \frac{p_i}{1 - p_i}.$$

Conveniently odds are not restricted to values from 0 to 1 but can range up to infinity.[64] This makes it easier to work with them during regressions, as values never can be too high. Nevertheless the problem of a lower bound still remains. This is fixed by taking the logarithm of these odds.[65] This logarithm of the odds now is fitted to a linear curve, comparable to the one already discussed during the normal OLSM. Nevertheless this time the explained variable is not a linear value but the logarithm of the odds.

$$\ln\frac{p}{1-p} = \beta_0 + \sum \beta_i \cdot x_i + u.$$

The parameters for the Logit-Model are not estimated using the 'least square method' used before, but are fitted via the 'maximum likelihood method'. This method uses several iterations to check for the best fitting model for the parameters and constantly compares the estimated models with the data.[66]

It goes without saying, that the interpretation of the model is not the same as was the case using the OLSM. Unfortunately the interpretation is now less intuitive and

---

64 As $\frac{0}{1} = 0$ and $\lim_{p\to 1}(\frac{p}{1-p}) \to \infty$.

65 $\lim_{x\to 0}(\ln x) = -\infty$, therefore no lower bound does remain.

66 The likelihood of a certain case is $p_i^{Y_i} \cdot (1 - p_i)^{1-Y_i}$, the total likelihood is the product of the likelihoods from all the cases in the data set.

needs some further remarks. The parameter β_i now denotes the change to the logarithm of the odds when x_i changes by one unit. As this is hard to visualise, the exponential functions of the parameters are better suited for interpretation. If $e^{\beta_i} > 1$, then the odds increase when x_i escalates and vice versa. As this increase regrettably applies to the odds and not to the probabilities, it is not possible to give statements about the size of the effect on the probabilities without knowing all the different variables. So it is necessary to take all other observable variables into account when trying to make statements about the implications of a Logit-Model.

During the discussion about the Contest Success Functions it emerged that the Difference Contest Success Function is a special case of the family of logistical functions. As the same is true for the Logit-Model, it is perfectly suited for conducting research on the DCSF. It is possible to convert it into its probability notion, $p = \frac{e^Z}{1+e^Z}$. Evidently this is the same as the Difference Contest Success Function in its two-player configuration.[67]

c. *Synopsis of the Estimators*

By learning about these two methods of conducting regression analysis we now are able to apply econometrics on the Contest Success Functions. On the one hand, we have been enabled to do a regression analysis with the Ratio CSF using the OLSM. We only have to keep in mind that although this still remains the easiest and most usable possibility for doing such a regression, several problems are probable to arise.

[67] The two-player case of the Difference Contest Success Function was defined as $p_1 = \frac{1}{1+e^{\gamma(c_2-c_1)}} = \frac{e^{-\gamma(c_2-c_1)}}{1+e^{-\gamma(c_2-c_1)}}$, so that by substituting $-\gamma \cdot (c_1 - c_2)$ for Z in the Logit-Model we can estimate the mass-effect-parameter γ within the Logit-Model easily.

On the other hand we now are capable of working with the Logit-Model to do empirical research by using the Difference Contest Success Function. Nevertheless, the complex interpretation needed by this model makes it somewhat harder to grasp and forces us to and to cope with a more extensive explanation. But for all that we have realised that the Logit-Models offers us several attributes that make it predestined for use with an explained variable with structural dichotomy.

7. Fitting the Ratio CSF via the Linear Probabilistic Model

During the course of the next two chapters we will apply the knowledge acquired about Contest Success Functions and empirical approaches to the actual data set. The following chapter will be concerned with fitting the Ratio CSF to the historical battles gathered. This is done via the Linear Probabilistic Model, which is the OLSM elaborated on in the last chapter when the explained variable is binary in nature. After the general approach has been sketched out the second part will cover the actual regressions and discuss their results.

a. *Approach and Parameters*

To do an empirical study we first have to consider the model we are using to do the regression on. The basic model is quite obvious in this case, as we want to discuss the applicability of the Ratio CSF on battles during the Napoleonic era. Therefore our basic model is the Ratio CSF.

$$p_i = \frac{(k_i c_i)^m}{\sum_{j=1}^{n} (k_j c_j)^m}$$

We have to start our analysis by asking what we do know about the model and especially what we do not know. Since we can only allude to what our data tells us, we only know about the size of the forces involved and Napoleon's presence on the battlefield. Given that the Ratio CSF does rely on the force sizes, we at least can assume that it can be applied here. Nevertheless a problem concerning the Ratio CSF is caused by what we do not know, which includes the size of the mass-effect-parameter m and the efficiency k_i of the different forces involved. As can be proven, for $m \neq 1$ we can not assume that including all the forces individually will yield the same effects as treating them as a coherent fighting force.[68]

Assuming that $m=1$ is a very harsh restriction since we do not know anything about it, so we have to base our further analysis on the two player case, where the French Army and the Coalition Forces are the two contestants. Rephrasing the Ratio CSF into the two-player case yields the following equation for the probability of success:

$$p_{Fr}=\frac{(k_{Fr}c_{Fr})^m}{(k_{Fr}c_{Fr})^m+(k_{Co}c_{Co})^m}$$

Without loosing any information we can simplify matters by dropping k_{Co} from this formula, hence fitting its value at 1. This only implies that we accept the efficiency of the Coalition Forces as being the standard of these times. The French efficiency is then rescaled, so that we now can compare the efficiencies pretty easily.

$$p_{Fr}=\frac{(\frac{k_{Fr}}{k_{Co}}c_{Fr})^m}{(\frac{k_{Fr}}{k_{Co}}c_{Fr})^m+(\frac{k_{Co}}{k_{Co}}c_{Co})^m}=\frac{(\frac{k_{Fr}}{k_{Co}}c_{Fr})^m}{(\frac{k_{Fr}}{k_{Co}}c_{Fr})^m+(c_{Co})^m}$$

$$\underset{\frac{k_{Fr}}{k_{Co}}=k}{\longrightarrow} p_{Fr}=\frac{(kc_{Fr})^m}{(kc_{Fr})^m+(c_{Co})^m}$$

Nevertheless we do not know how big m and k actually are. However it is possible to approximate k employing a numerical approach exemplified in Appendix C, using iterative regressions, fed by the results of the previous one.

---

68 Proof is pretty obvious, as $p_i=\frac{(k_ic_i)^m}{\sum_j(k_jc_j)^m}\neq\frac{(k_ic_i)^m}{\left[\sum_{j\neq i}(k_jc_j)\right]^m+(k_ic_i)^m}$ for all $m\neq1$.

Concerning m, there is no way to know beforehand which value will yield the best results. Moreover, every non-negative value is possibly the correct one to describe the Ratio CSF and so no value can be excluded by recurring on theory. Hence it is not enough to do one regression, but imperative to conduct a series of regression with different m in a plausible range. Furthermore, we still have to integrate the effect of Napoleon into our estimator, as the working hypothesis states that he actually had impact on the outcome of the battles. There are several ways to integrate this binary variable, but three stand out as being the most probable from a theoretical point of view.

Firstly, we could visualise Napoleon to have an overall impact on the whole battle. This impact would be the same, regardless how big the forces involved would actually be. Secondly, one can think of a model where Napoleon had an impact on the value of every French soldier under his command, adding a specific value to k. The third model would be one, in which both effects could be measured, so that the chance of winning a battle would be increased by a fixed percentage on Napoleon's presence and furthermore the k of the forces would be affected as well. This leaves us with four models we have to consider, as Napoleon could be without impact as well.

Model 1: *No effect of Napoleon*

$$p_{Fr} = \beta_1 EffortRatio + u$$

Model 2: *Fixed effect*

$$p_{Fr} = \beta_1 EffortRatio + \beta_2 Nap + u$$

Model 3: *Effects on every soldier*

$$p_{Fr} = \beta_1 \cdot (1 - Nap) \cdot EffortRatio + \beta_2 \cdot Nap \cdot EffortRatio + u$$

Model 4: *Effects on every soldier and fixed effect*

$$p_{Fr} = \beta_1 \cdot (1 - Nap) \cdot EffortRatio + \beta_2 \cdot Nap \cdot EffortRatio + \beta_3 Nap + u$$

Testing different models is without any value if we do not know how to judge and rank them. As was shown in the previous chapter a linear regression via the OLSM is not optimal due to the dichotomy of winning or loosing a battle. Especially we anticipated the model to have fairly high residuals, because estimated probabilities, except for the case of 0 and 1, never are without a difference from the actual outcomes. This is why the common approach of using the so-called R^2 is of considerably less worth than it would have been if the dichotomy of data would not be present. R^2 is a coefficient of determination, which gives the proportion of variation in a data set that is accounted for by the model specified. When using the Linear Probabilistic Model and doing regression on an explained binary variable, residuals have to appear and R^2 will always be rather low. Using R^2 to judge how good a fit has been obtained hence is not reasonable.[69]

When there are only two possible outcomes and we want to predict the probability of winning for a certain two-player contest, there is a much more accessible concept for a good fit: The ratio of the correct predictions and the sum of all of them. This gives us the percentage of how often the model did offer us the correct predictions and hence is very easy to grasp. A correct prediction would be if the model predicts

69 Consider the case where a model correctly predicts all outcomes when divided at the 0.5 level. This model could have a very low R^2 while still doing all we want it to do. Now think of a model where three of the predicted values would be different, two being slightly smaller, so giving wrong predictions but with nearly the same residuals and one predicting an exact fit of 1. The R^2 of this model would be higher, although the predictive value would be lower. Hence R^2 can be no applicable measure for the fit of a model when dichotomy applies.

$p > 0.5$, which means that the probability of winning the contest is bigger than the probability of loosing it. We shall use this ratio from now on to measure the fit of a model, especially as this concept will be easy to extend to the Logit-Model and the Difference CSF, which are analysed in the next chapter. By employing this easy approach the goodness of fit can be compared between totally different models and even different ways of conducting the regression analysis.

We now have constructed four different models we need to compare. This comparison will tell us if Ratio CSF can be applied on this particular set of historic battles and we will see how good the fit of the different models actually is. Furthermore the influence of Napoleon on the performance of French troops can be scrutinized and – if this influence materialises – quantified.

b. *Interpretation*

To interpret the results we have to analyse every model on its own before comparing them. The extensive information for each model is available in Appendix D, in each case together with a plot of the fits[70] for specific cases of m.

Model 1: *No effect of Napoleon*

$p_{Fr} = \beta_1 EffortRatio + u$

The highest fit for Model 1 is reached when $m_1 = 0.92$ and has the value of 60.09%. As we only run the regression on the ratio of efforts we do get only one coefficient. This is highly significant, so that we can reject the hypothesis that $h_o : \beta_1 = 0$.

[70] At the plots the value 'fit' does denote the ratio of wrong results and all the estimates.

The result of the regression does fit in plausibly with the theory of the Ratio CSF as $\beta_1 = 0.98956$ nearly equals 1, hence the French and the Coalition Forces are of nearly equal fighting value in this model.

Model 2: *Fixed effect*

$$p_{Fr} = \beta_1 EffortRatio + \beta_2 Nap + u$$

The second model, which does include the ratio of efforts as well as a fixed effect upon Napoleon's presence, achieves its best results at $m_2 = 2.41$. The fit at this level is 69.17%, which is slightly smaller than the one employing Model 1. Interpretation of Model 2 is somewhat harder since the effort ratio must be calculated while considering the value m_2 as well. The model estimates the French to fight with 68.14% of the fighting value the coalition could muster, which would not be consistent with history.[71] Napoleon's presence on the battlefield would have been worth a 34.627% increase in the probability of winning according to the model, which is a very high score. Nevertheless $h_o : \beta_1 = 0$ and $h_o : \beta_2 = 0$ can both be rejected, even at the 0.001 level.

Model 3: *Effects on every soldier*

$$p_{Fr} = \beta_1 \cdot (1 - Nap) \cdot EffortRatio + \beta_2 \cdot Nap \cdot EffortRatio + u$$

The third model includes as variables the ratio of efforts for both Napoleon's absence and his presence on the battlefield. Boosting its fit of 69.92% at a level of $m_3 = 1.17$, it both has the highest fit and R^2 of the models tested. Both coefficients are highly significant and easily accessible to

---

71 Calculation:

$$\beta_1 = k^m$$
$$\mapsto 0.3082707 = k^{2.41}$$
$$\mapsto k = 0.6814$$

interpretation. The model estimates that without Napoleon's presence the French soldiers fought with 74.4% of the comparative value of Coalition forces. This would have increased to 109,13% if Napoleon was the commander in chief of the French forces. Napoleon then would have increased the efficiency of each soldier by 46.68%.

Model 4: *Effects on every soldier and fixed effect*

$$p_{Fr} = \beta_1 \cdot (1 - Nap) \cdot EffortRatio + \beta_2 \cdot Nap \cdot EffortRatio + \beta_3 Nap + u$$

At last Model 4 has to be considered, which merges Model 2 and Model 3. We thus are enabled to compare these easier by means of a model comparative to both of them. The best fit with an accuracy of 67.67% for this model can be gained by using $m_4 = 1.07$. Values up to 1.25 will yield the same results as long as we are concerned only with an optimal fit. Interestingly this is the only model where some hypotheses can be rejected. $\beta_1 = 0.72234$ translates to a 73.78% efficiency of French soldiers without Napoleon and $\beta_2 = 0.92237$ to 92.73% efficiency with him being the commander in chief. Furthermore the model predicts an additional increase of $\beta_3 = 0.14242$ in the winning probability if Napoleon was present.

While $h_o : \beta_1 = 0$ can be rejected even when the highest standards are to be maintained, the same can not be said of $h_o : \beta_2 = 0$ and $h_o : \beta_3 = 0$. Nevertheless there are reasonable confidence intervals so that $h_o : \beta_2 = 0$ can be rejected – even the 10% confidence interval is enough. This argumentation is not possible for $h_o : \beta_3 = 0$, hence an independent influence of a fixed effect is not supported by Model 4.

Conclusion

There will always be some battles a model will predict wrongly. Chance and human behaviour are influential when the outcome of models is predicted. A bad day of the general in charge or a brilliant spark of his adversary can decide which side will win the struggle. Nevertheless there are some conclusions the different models have to offer if their analyses are combined.

1. Obviously Model 3 had the highest predictive value, both in terms of goodness of fit and the somewhat obsolete R^2.

2. For Model 4 we are not able to reject $h_o : \beta_3 = 0$ for reasonable values. Hence the fixed effect of Napoleon seems doubtable.

3. Three of the models (1, 3 and 4) work best with m near to 1. Only Model 2 argues for another m, but this is most likely due to the fixed effect of Napoleon's presence warping the results for the ratio of efforts.

4. As Model 3 is an enhanced version of Model 1 we would expect β_1 and β_2 to be roughly the same. Nevertheless this is not the case. Hence Model 3 seems to be superior to Model 1.[72]

All of this taken into account, the model which describes the battles of the Napoleonic era the best is number 3. Thus we do conclude the following concerning the applicability of the Ratio CSF:

[72] As the variances of the different variables are not independent but depend on the values of the other variables it is not possible without problems to employ standard t-tests. Nevertheless the confidence intervals of β_1 and β_2 do not overlap at the 0.05 significance level when standard t-tests are used.

1. The Ratio CSF can be applied.
2. Napoleon definitely had a significant impact on the probabilities.
3. The best description for this impact is an increase of 46.68% on the fighting ability of each French soldier.
4. The Ratio CSF is capable of giving predictions with up to 69.92% accuracy.

8. Fitting the Difference CSF via the Logit-Model

As discussed before, there are two Contest Success Functions, both of which are widely discussed among scholars of economic science. The first one is the Ratio CSF exemplified during the last chapter, which works by linking the probability of winning a contest to the ratio of the efforts put into it by a particular contestant and the input of all the players. The second approach is the so-called Difference CSF, which does not link the ratio of the efforts to the chance of winning but the difference between the efforts. This concept already has been theoretically elaborated before and will be put to use during the course or this chapter. Firstly, we will consider what we do know and how we could describe the model, so that we can estimate it via the Logit-Model. Secondly, the actual regressions are run and compared.

a. *Approach and Parameters*

We start by considering the Difference CSF already established in the theoretical part of this thesis. The probability of success then can be expressed as:

$$p_i = \frac{e^{\gamma \cdot k_i \cdot c_i}}{\sum_{j=1}^{n} e^{\gamma \cdot k_j \cdot c_j}}$$

It is now imperative to establish what we do know about the model and how to use this knowledge to model probabilities correctly. As was the case when analysing the Ratio CSF and the Linear Probabilistic Model, we do know about the force sizes of the contestants and about Napoleon's presence on the battlefield. To apply the Difference CSF we only do need to know about the force sizes, hence it can be used with the information provided by the data set.

Conveniently we can integrate the different coalition forces into the Difference CSF without blending them into one simple variable. Instead we can use the size of every sub-force and hence obtain estimates not only about the combined efficiency of Napoleon's adversaries, but about every single nation involved in the struggle.[73] We thus expect this model to predict better results and give us a better fit.

Judging the goodness of fit for a Logit-Model shares some of the difficulties we encountered using the Linear Probabilistic Model. There does exists a Pseudo-R^2, but it can only tell us which model predicts more of variance in a data set if one model is a simplified version of the other one. For this reason it would be possibly to compare only some models with each other, thus not permitting to drop one model totally. The best way to judge how good a model works for our historical data actually is the same we already employed before: The ratio of correctly predicted and total battles.

For the standard formula of the Logit-Model[74] we now can postulate the four different models, which are similarly constructed to the ones scrutinized via the Ratio CSF:

Model 1: *No effect of Napoleon*[75]

$$\ln\frac{p}{1-p} = \beta_{Fr}FrFor + \sum_i \beta_i EnFor_i + u$$

---

73 $\ln\frac{p}{1-p} = \beta_0 \cdot ForFr + \beta_1 \cdot ForCo + u$ describes the Logit-Model for two players. We can then substitute $\beta_1 \cdot ForCo$ with $\beta_{Br}For_{Br} + \beta_{Rus}For_{Rus} + \beta_{Pr}For_{Pr} + \ldots$, this way these parameters describing the particular sub forces of the coalition army have been integrated into the whole model. Furthermore this is easy to understand if the influence of the coefficients is considered, which is e^{β} on the odds and is given per soldier.

74 $\ln\frac{p}{1-p} = \beta_0 + \sum \beta_i \cdot x_i + u$

75 Where $\sum_i \beta_i EnFor_i$ is the sum of the efforts of the French enemies present.

Model 2: *Fixed effect*

$$\ln\frac{p}{1-p} = \beta_{Fr} FrFor + \sum_i \beta_i EnFor_i + \beta_{Nap} Nap + u$$

Model 3: *Effects on every soldier*

$$\ln\frac{p}{1-p} = (1 - Nap)\cdot \beta_{Fr} \cdot FrFor + Nap\cdot \beta_{NapFr} \cdot FrFor + \sum_i \beta_i EnFor_i + u$$

Model 4: *Effects on every soldier and fixed effect*

$$\ln\frac{p}{1-p} = (1 - Nap)\cdot \beta_{Fr} \cdot FrFor + Nap\cdot \beta_{NapFr} \cdot FrFor + \sum_i \beta_i EnFor_i + \beta_{NapFr} \cdot Nap + u$$

We now have again constructed four models which could describe the functional relationship between force sizes, Napoleon's presence and the probability for winning the battle. It now remains to test the four models and to interpret the results obtained.

b. Interpretation

Before comparing the different models we again have to analyse them independently. The extensive information for each model is available in Appendix G, so that all the results can be verified.

Model 1: *No effect of Napoleon*

$$\ln\frac{p}{1-p} = \beta_{Fr} FrFor + \sum_i \beta_i EnFor_i + u$$

The simplest Difference CSF model used provides a fit of 72.18%, which is higher than the best fit of all the Ratio CSF models we tested in the previous chapter. Furthermore we obtain probable results with all the e^{β}, the effect on the odds, staying near 1, which is consistent both with theory and history. Whereas the effects for the French, British, Russian and Austrian forces are highly significant, the coefficient for the Prussians is less so – the effects for the Spanish & Portuguese forces and the contingent of the several smaller German nations can not be considered significant for reasonable significance levels.

Model 2: *Fixed effect*

$$\ln\frac{p}{1-p} = \beta_{Fr}FrFor + \sum_i \beta_i EnFor_i + \beta_{Nap}Nap + u$$

The fixed effect model includes a specific effect Napoleon had upon him taking command of the fielded French forces. This boosts the ratio of correctly predicted results to 74.43%, thus increasing slightly from the model without Napoleon. Nearly the same significance levels are obtained, thus only the fixed effect has to be reconsidered. Scoring significance even at the 95% level it supports the theory that Napoleon had an impact on the battlefield.

Model 3: *Effects on every soldier*

$$\ln\frac{p}{1-p} = (1-Nap)\cdot \beta_{Fr}\cdot FrFor + Nap\cdot \beta_{NapFr}\cdot FrFor + \sum_i \beta_i EnFor_i + u$$

Comparable to the models tested that were based on the Ratio CSF, Model 3 produces the best fit for the Difference CSF as well. 76.69% of battles are correctly predicted by this model. Furthermore all parameters, with the exception of the Spanish & Portuguese and the cumulated further nations, are highly significant at least at the 95% significance level. This underpins the high predictive value of this model even more.

Model 4: *Effects on every soldier and fixed effect*

$$\ln\frac{p}{1-p} = (1 - Nap)\cdot \beta_{Fr}\cdot FrFor + Nap\cdot \beta_{NapFr}\cdot FrFor + \sum_i \beta_i EnFor_i + \beta_{NapFr}\cdot Nap + u$$

The fourth model has a slightly decreased fit value compared to Model 3, with 75.94% of all battles anticipated with the correct result. Furthermore, the significance levels are lower for the coefficients describing the impact of the separate forces. Compared with Model 2, the fixed effect of Napoleon when his effects on the single soldiers has been controlled for is roughly cut by two third of its impact on the odds. Anymore, the fixed effect of Napoleon is insignificant and could only be admitted at a 10% significance level – this makes the whole effect very doubtable.

Conclusion

As we have analysed, there are several features among the four models worth emphasizing:

1. The effects for the Spanish & Portuguese Forces and the contingents of the smaller German states are not significant in any of the models.

2. All the models based on the Difference CSF provide us with a higher predictive value than any of the ones build upon the Ratio CSF.

3. When the effects of Napoleon for every single French soldier are controlled, there remains no significant evidence for a fixed effect applying as well.

4. The effects for the armies of all great powers are significant. Their significance even improves when the effects of Napoleon on single soldiers is accounted for.

Taking these four points into account, we can think of a fifth model based on the Difference CSF which includes Napoleon's effect on each soldiers while omitting a fixed effect. In addition, the forces of Spain/Portugal and the minor German countries are not included into the model because they have been shown to be not significant in any of the four models employed before. This leaves us with the following model:

Model 5: *Effects on every soldier, no SP and UN*

$$\ln\frac{p}{1-p} = \begin{bmatrix} \beta_{Br}\cdot BrFor + \beta_{pr}\cdot \Pr For + \beta_{Rus}\cdot RusFor + \beta_{Aus}\cdot AusFor + \\ (1-Nap)\cdot \beta_{Fr}\cdot FrFor + Nap\cdot \beta_{NapFr}\cdot FrFor \end{bmatrix} + u$$

As can be seen in Appendix G, this refined model provides us with the best fit encountered among all the models, be they Ratio CSF or Difference CSF models. We can predict 78.20% of the battle results correctly when this model is employed. As is evident from the data we obtain high significance values for all the parameters included, thus verifying the robustness of this approach.

The size of the effects for the forces is consistent with what we believe to know about warfare as well. While the French forces presence increases the odds of a French victory all the different nations fighting among the coalition forces decrease these. In addition, the performance of the French troops under Napoleon's command is predicted to be substantially higher than when he was not present.

Considering what we just ascertained about the fifth model we can infer from the findings of the chapter the following:

1. The Difference CSF can be applied.[76]

2. Again we have ascertained a highly significant impact of Napoleon on both the odds and the probabilities of winning a battle.

3. A general description of this impact is not possible, as the exact percentage of it depends on all the factors involved. To nevertheless put the impact into perspective we can consider a battle with 10,000 French troops. Were Napoleon present he would improve the odds of a French victory by the factor 1.50.[77]

4. The Difference CSF models are capable of giving predictions with an accuracy of up to 78.20%.

---

76 Which is quite trivial, as every model could have been used. Nevertheless the predictive value is much higher than what guessing could have achieved.

77 Always keeping in mind that this increase is not proportional to how the probabilities change.

9. Ratio Or Difference CSF? – Comparing The Results

As seen during the course of this thesis, both the Ratio CSF and the Difference CSF provide us with applicable estimators for the probability of success in battle. Nevertheless, the two most prominent models of each CSF need to be set in contrast to provide us with a definitive result about the working hypotheses. Answering the questions about the applicability of CSF on battles and Napoleon's influence on his forces is not possible without singling out the best model beforehand.

a. *Decision Time: The Best Model*

Both the Ratio and the Difference CSF had the best fit when no fixed effect of Napoleon was presumed but when we checked for the effects of his presence on every single soldier. Nevertheless there are several differences between the two models.

1. Firstly, there is a difference in which approach is used to model the function. We discussed the different implications of the Ratio and the Difference CSF in detail during previous chapters and we should keep in mind, that the assumption about a homogeneous battlefield and stable conditions put forth by the Ratio CSF during our thoughts on the combat can not be guaranteed. In fact, they are highly doubtable for the real data.

2. The Ratio CSF contains only the French forces, the size of the coalition army and Napoleon himself as explanatory variables. This provides us with no way to correct for different force efficiency among the allied countries. Contrary to these restrictions on the Ratio CSF, the Difference CSF enables us to provide individual coefficients

for the several fighting countries as well. Although the values for two allies could not be proven to be of significance, coefficients for all great-powers could be established.

3. We could only expect the Ratio CSF to give us predictive values for all the powers involved if the data set would include a fair amount of battles fought by each power without their respective allies present. A model making use of this approach was established but proved to give even worse results. This is not true for the Difference CSF, as the different forces can be included without problems.

4. By minimising the sum of the squared residuals, the OLSM predictor used to obtain results for the Ratio CSF actually can worsen the predictive value during dichotomy if more variables are included. This is not likely to happen for the 'Maximum-Likelihood-Approach' of the Logit-Model.

5. Furthermore the fit values obtained for every model constructed via the Difference CSF were superior to the ones of every model using the Ratio CSF. Model 3 of the Ratio CSF predicted 50% more faulty outcomes than the comparable model based on the Difference CSF.

6. All the models are superior to a simple estimation where the superior force is expected to win all the times, as this model only has a fit of 60.9%. Thus all the models explain more than a prosaic rule of thumb does, we therefore can judge all the models to at least partially explain the imponderability of combat.

7. The models using the Ratio approach do not always predict values in a 0 to 1 range. Hence some of the values have to

be changed if an interpretation as predictions about the battle outcomes is aspired. The Difference CSF produces only results that are valid and between 0 and 1.

8. During the Napoleonic wars most generals never put up a fight if they were numerically inferior. Hence most of the battles have force differences at levels of 5,000 or less soldiers. As the sizes of the armies were mostly in excess of 30,000 soldiers on each side, the ratio of forces during most battles was not lower than approximately 45%. Thus using this ratio as explanatory variable is troublesome because the variance in the variable is rather small. The Difference CSF – contrary to the name - is not troubled by this, as the forces are not divided by the overall size of the armies fighting. Furthermore the Difference CSF exactly was created to describe circumstances where the force sizes would roughly be equal and small changes could have significant results.

Taking all that was said beforehand into account it emerges, that the Difference CSF describes the battles fought during the Napoleonic era much better than the Ratio CSF. These findings are fortified by both theoretical analysis and the actual results. Thus we conclude that the battles of the Napoleonic age are best predicted by applying models based upon the Difference CSF.

b. Interpretation Of the Best Model

We now have established that the Difference CSF should be used for modelling the battles of this era. Of the models we tested, the fifth one provided us with the best predictive results, making correct guesses for nearly 80% of the observations. This clearly made it stand out from among the models we have obtained. Nevertheless the effects and coefficients of this model are not so easy to grasp since the Logit-Model is not very intuitive at first sight.

We have to start by taking a closer look at the coefficients. As these do not change the odds directly but are incorporated into a power, we first have to transform the Logit-Model. The shape we need is one where the power that includes all the coefficients is segregated into the individual effects.[78]

Using the data set obtained by the historical research we then can estimate all the e^{β} terms:

$e^{\beta_{Br}}$	= 0.9997945	British Forces
$e^{\beta_{Pr}}$	= 0.9999546	Prussian Forces
$e^{\beta_{Rus}}$	= 0.9999355	Russian Forces
$e^{\beta_{Aus}}$	= 0.9999664	Austrian Forces
$e^{\beta_{Fr}}$	= 1.0000335	French Forces
$e^{\beta_{Nap}}$	= 1.0000743	French Forces when Napoleon was present

This enables us to compute the actual estimator for the odds of a French victory. Not dealing with the model any more but with the coefficients we obtained, we have to drop the unpredictable and not observable influence of u. This is possible because we expect the mean of this error term to be zero, i. e. $E[u]=0$. By fitting the estimated e^{β} values into the model we get the estimator of odds.

$$E[Odds_{VFr}] = 1.0000335^{(1-Nap)\cdot ForFr} \cdot 1.0000743^{Nap\cdot ForFr} \cdot 0.9997945^{ForBr} \cdot 0.9999546^{For\,Pr} \cdot 0.9999355^{ForRus} \cdot 0.9999664^{Aus}$$

78 The odds of a French victory are:

$$\frac{p}{1-p} = e^{\beta_{Br}\cdot BrFor + \beta_{pr}\cdot \Pr For + \beta_{Rus}\cdot RusFor + \beta_{Aus}\cdot AusFor + (1-Nap)\cdot\beta_{Fr}\cdot FrFor + Nap\cdot\beta_{NapFr}\cdot FrFor + u}$$

$$\frac{p}{1-p} = e^{\beta_{Br}\cdot BrFor} \cdot e^{\beta_{Pr}\cdot \Pr For} \cdot e^{\beta_{Rus}\cdot RusFor} \cdot e^{\beta_{Aus}\cdot AusFor} \cdot e^{(1-Nap)\cdot\beta_{Fr}\cdot FrFor} \cdot e^{Nap\cdot\beta_{Nap}\cdot FrFor} \cdot e^{u}$$

It now is obvious how changes in the explanatory variables affect the odds for a French victory. Whenever a further French soldier is added to the battle, the odds for a French victory are increased by the factor 1.0000335. Whenever a French soldier under Napoleon's command is added, we have an increase by factor 1.0000743. Correspondingly the factor for the enemy forces have to be treated – the only difference is that they reduce the odds of a French victory instead of increasing them. This makes it possible for us to compare the efficiency of the different nations. Figure 5 shows how the efficiencies compare to each other as their ratios.

	Br	Pr	Rus	Aus	Fr	Nap
Br		1,000160132907	1,000141028981	1,000171935333	1,000172036476	1,000131232488
Pr	0,999839892731		0,999980899133	1,000011800536	1,000011901663	0,999971104208
Rus	0,999858990005	1,000019101232		1,000030901993	1,000031003122	0,999990204888
Aus	0,999828094224	0,999988199604	0,999969098962		1,000000101126	0,999959304153
Fr	0,999827993116	0,999988098479	0,999968997839	0,999999898874		0,999959203031
Nap	0,999868784731	1,000028896627	1,000009795208	1,000040697504	1,000040798633	

Figure 5. Ratios of the Effects on the Odds

There are some interesting interrelations that can be detected in this table. Obviously the British forces have been estimated as being superior to all the other ones. Surprisingly they are even considered to be better than French soldiers fighting under the command of Napoleon. As only one battle could be included where both Napoleon and British forces had been present, we should not emphasize this singularity too much.

The French performance without Napoleon is surprisingly bad. Underperforming against every enemy we would not expect them to hold out very long on their own. Here further historical research would be needed to check if the French troops commanded by Napoleon and the one he did not have under his direct control have been inhomogeneous.[79]

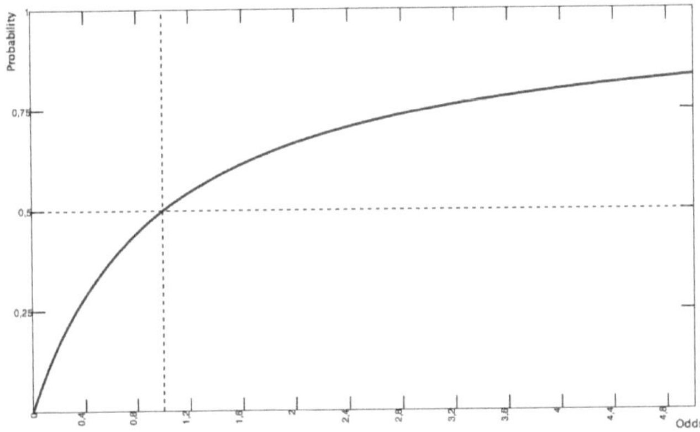

Figure 6. Relation of Odds and Probability

The results for Napoleon are not surprising. He outperforms all the other great powers, especially the French troops that were not under his command.[80] Nevertheless the performance of his troops did not depend on him alone, but includes also the same effect we encountered among the French troops. Hence we have to control for the effect the French troops do have on the odds. As the French e^{β} is 1.0000335 and the e^{β} of the forces under Napoleons command 1.0000743, we have to divide this through the former to quantify the influence of Napoleon alone. The result is 1.000040799, which is the factor by which the odds of a French victory were improved by Napoleon's presence *for every soldier under his command.* Hence the total effect of Napoleon was a factor of $1.000040799^{FrForces}$, by which the

[79] As the best troops always stayed under direct command of Napoleon and he commanded the most important battles by himself, this could well explain the meagre performance of French troops without him.

[80] Except for the British troops. But as already has been mentioned before these results are not truly comparable because they were constructed using only one observation.

odds were multiplied. Although this may seem small at a first glance, the power laws let this factor grow exponentially with the size of the French forces. His presence effectively doubled the French odds for every 17,000 French soldiers present.

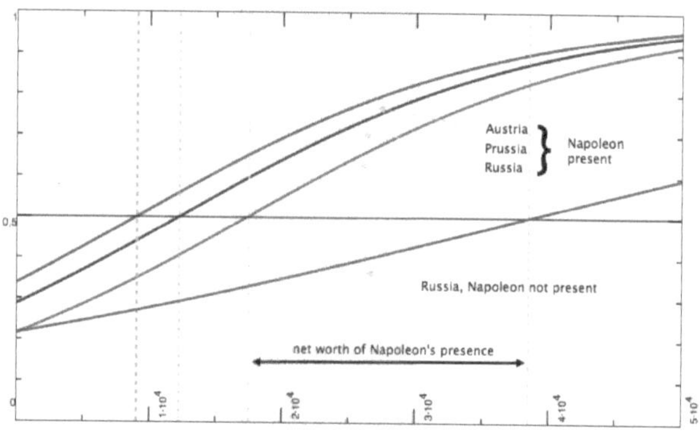

Figure 7. Probability of Winning for French Forces fighting 20,000 Enemies with and without Napoleon present

To put Napoleon's performance into the context of the actual probability of winning, we have to understand how the odds and the probability are connected. As the definition of the odds is $Odds = p/_{1-p}$ we can transpose this to $p = Odds/_{1+Odds}$. The first order derivative of this is $\frac{\partial p}{\partial Odds} = 1/_{(1+Odds)^2}$, which is strictly positive for all positive odds. Nevertheless we have to be aware that the increase is not constant but depends on the value of the odds. Thus doubling the odds is not equivalent to doubling the probability of success. As the odds depend on the present forces, the net value of Napoleon can only be assessed if the force levels of his enemies and his army are taken into account.

As we are especially interested in the performance of Napoleon and his troops, we will exemplify these relations via an example and a graphical interpretation. Figure 7 provides us with four graphs, which link the size of the French forces to their probability of winning of which the upper three include the effects of Napoleon on his troops while the lower one does not. For all four probability graphs the enemy fielded 20,000 troops. Even when fighting against the quite efficient Russians, Napoleon needed less than half the amount of troops a less competent general had to field to qualify for a 50% probability of winning the battle. In fact the net worth of Napoleon's presence would have been 20,987 French soldiers.

IV Résumé

It is very true that I have said that I considered Napoleon's presence in the field equal to forty thousand men in the balance. This is a very loose way of talking; but the idea is a very different one from that of his presence at a battle being equal to a reinforcement of forty thousand men.

Arthur Wellesley, 1. Duke of Wellington

10. How much was Napoleon actually worth?

Providing case studies is an important method to visualise the effects decisions and actions can have in economic theory. The Contest Success Functions evolved when economists tried to evolve a theory that would give correct predictions about actual conflicts. These early era already saw many examples, thus three case studies will be used to exemplify what the model developed in this thesis is able to explain.

a. 40,000 Soldiers

The idea for this thesis evolved when the author stumbled upon a quote of Wellington about Napoleon. Although unverified, it stimulated thought on the topic of Napoleonic warfare and empirical research:

> 'I used to say of him [Napoleon] that his presence on the field made the difference of forty thousand men.'

This case study will now answer when – according to the model established before – Napoleon's presence made this drastic difference. For a start we have to consider what 40,000 men difference really means. Obviously we can state that Napoleon had the effect of 40,000 men if his probability to win a certain conflict were exactly the same when compared to a typical French general commanding 40,00 men more in battle. When the probabilities are to be the same, then the odds and their logarithms necessarily also have to be. Thus we have the following equation that has to be fulfilled if we want Napoleon to have the desired effect:

$$\ln\frac{p}{1-p} = \beta_{Fr} \cdot (FrForces) + \sum \beta_i \cdot x_i = \beta_{Nap} \cdot (FrForces - 40{,}000) + \sum \beta_i \cdot x_i$$

Necessarily the effects of the other forces cancel themselves out. Napoleon's superiority is constant in this model and hence his edge does not depend on how big the enemy forces are, but only on how big we want the gap between him and the other general to be. Thus we can transpose the equation to:

$$\beta_{Fr} \cdot (FrForces) = \beta_{Nap} \cdot (FrForces - 40{,}000)$$

$$\beta_{Fr} \cdot FrForces = \beta_{Nap} \cdot FrForces - \beta_{Nap} \cdot 40{,}000$$

$$\beta_{Nap} \cdot 40{,}000 = (\beta_{Nap} - \beta_{Fr}) \cdot FrForces$$

$$\rightarrow FrForces = \frac{\beta_{Nap} \cdot 40{,}000}{\beta_{Nap} - \beta_{Fr}}$$

Since $\beta_{Nap} = 0.00007435$ and $\beta_{Fr} = 0.00003352$ we calculate that for Napoleon to be worth an extra 40,000 troops 32,838 French soldiers would have been needed under his command. Now this seems to be an exceptionally low number. The mean of the forces employed by Napoleon was 56,308 soldiers, if we exclude the biggest battles only 41,919 Frenchmen. Hence this estimate by the Duke of Wellington actually was quite good when used only as a rough measure of Napoleon's worth.

b. Jena and Auerstedt, October 14th 1806

Jena and Auerstedt are two battles of high importance in Prussian History. They mark the disintegration of the army that Frederick the Great used to sweep through Silesia twice and that saved Prussia from annihilation during the Seven Years War. Thus the two battles are synonymous with how rotten the Kingdom of Prussia had become during the long peace.

At Jena Napoleon Bonaparte could muster ca 54,000 men out of his main army of 96,000.[81] The allied commander, General Prince Hohenlohe-Ingelfingen, only had 45,000 soldiers at his hand to defend against the meticulously planned attack of Napoleon's forces. Meanwhile at Auerstedt Davouts corps of roughly 30,000 French soldiers had to cope with 52,000 Prussians. Bernadotte, who was in viewing distance, could have intervened but decided not to – getting a rebuke from Napoleon later for this indifference.

Though Napoleon's victory was fairly reasonable with a predicted probability of 87.77%, the same is not to be said about the battle at Auerstedt. With only a 20.60% chance of winning the battle, Davout put up a fine performance and not only managed to fight the Prussians back, but later even routed them. With the probabilities so low it does not wonder that Napoleon later was angry with Bernadotte for not intervening, as this would have increased the probability of winning to 33.66%. Davout earned his title of Duke of Auerstedt on this day.

c. *Austerlitz, December 2nd 1805*

The Battle of the Three Emperors, as the Battle of Austerlitz is known as well, is considered to be one of Napoleon's greatest victories and put the Third Coalition into shambles. The culmination of his sweep towards Ulm and beyond saw Napoleon deploying ca 50,000 infantry soldiers and 15,000 men in his cavalry units. On the other side Czar Alexander I of Russia, who was in command, could count on about 70,000 infantry and 16,500 cavalry, roughly 70% of the whole being Russian units.[82]

---

81 All the forces are taken from Smith (1998), pp. 223.

82 Smith (1998), pp. 215.

The model tells us that the battle was very even sided, the French probability for winning estimated at 52.12% with Napoleon in command. Without him the model predicts only a 7.12% of winning the battle. This tellingly confirms this battle as one of Napoleon's greatest,[83] as he changed the outcome from a sure loss to a victory with impressive results by his presence. Furthermore this explains why the allied commanders were sure of their victory. The model acquired by empirics and the historical research thus come to the same conclusion concerning the Battle of Austerlitz.

---

[83] Uffindell (2003), p. 25.

11. Final Consideration and Summary

The start of this thesis was formed by two working hypotheses. Firstly, that the battles of the Napoleonic era could be modelled via the Contest Success Functions and secondly, that Napoleon was superior to his peers and that his influence could be empirically quantified and proven to be existent.

To answer these questions, we first familiarised ourselves with the economic conflict theory and the different concepts for making predictions about the outcomes of conflicts. We then learned the ropes about the two different Conflict Success Functions by Tullock and Hirsleifer – the Ratio and the Difference Contest Success Function. Special importance rested on the question what kind of conflicts these models could be applicable to.

During the second part of the thesis, the general conditions of history and the data set were scrutinized. During the historical part it was elaborated which conditions would need to be included into the final model and whether homogeneity among the different warring parties would allow us any kind of comparison at all. Subsequently the data set was introduced and the observations explicated. Several possible problems with the data set were discussed and proven to be of no importance for the following empirical research.

We then went through the stages of modelling and fitting different alternatives for predicting the outcome of a battle in the Napoleonic era. We distinguished two different estimators, which could be used to fit the two Contest Success Functions. By trying both approaches we then gained several models which we judged afterwards, discussing their respective fit to the problem, their explaining variables and their mechanics. It emerged that both ways – though vastly different in how they were constructed and how they had to be calculated – led to the same results on how Napoleon's influence is to be integrated. Furthermore all the models showed that Napoleon's presence was highly significant. We then compared the results of the two analyses and concluded, that a Difference CSF, with Napoleon's influence modelled as an effect on the fighting ability of the individual soldiers, describes the battles pretty accurately with a ratio of 78.20% correctnes.

Thus have we not only shown that Contest Success Functions can be applied to battles, but also that the predictive value is very high, even if only the force sizes are known. Furthermore Napoleon's influence on the contest was accentuated and empirically proven to be existent.

Taking a comprehensive look at the steps described above and their respective results, *we can embrace that the two working hypotheses have been proven*:

1. The *applicability of the Contest Success Functions is evident*, as all of the models tested had a substantially higher predictive value than a simpleton approach of 'the bigger force wins'. In fact the Difference CSF as used in Model 5 was able to predict nearly 80% of the battle outcomes correctly. This implies as well that the Difference CSF has greater explanatory value when battles and not whole wars are analysed than the Ratio CSF.

2. The same *positive conclusion is true for the influence of Napoleon* on the outcome of the

battles. Every Model tested showed significance for Napoleon's presence, thus we can conclude that his abilities as a general were different from the skills of his peer group and in fact increased the probability of a positive outcome for the French forces substantially.

Without a doubt there still remain follow-up questions which only further research can answer.[84] But irrespective of these the goal of this thesis has been achieved, as both hypotheses could be proven and the empirical foundation of the Contest Success Functions be enlarged.

---

84 It would most certainly be very interesting to expand the temporal scope to the whole 18th century, especially since data on battles of these times would be adequately accessible as well. The same goes for including the clashes of Napoleonic times into a separate analysis, especially as during these clashes the force differences varied much more than at normal battles. Thus the Ratio CSF could be tested with a higher variance in the force ratio.

Bibliography

Books

Blanning, T.C.W. (1996): *The French Revolutionary Wars*. London: Hodder Arnold.

Chandler, D. (2001): *The Art of Warfare on Land*. London: Penguin.

Delbrück, H. (2000): *Geschichte der Kriegskunst*. Berlin: de Gruyter.

Dixit, A.; Nalebuff, B. (2008): *The Art of Strategy*. New York: W. W. Norton & Company.

Dupuy, T. N. (1979): *Numbers, Predictions and War*. London: Mcdonald and Jane's.

Elting, J.; Esposito, V.J. (1999): *A Military History and Atlas of the Napoleonic Wars*. London: Greenhill Books.

Fisher, T. (2004)a: *The Napoleonic Wars: Rise of the Emperor, 1805-1807 v. 1*. Oxford: Osprey Publishing.

Fisher, T. (2004)b: *The Napoleonic Wars: Empires Fight Back 1808-1812 v. 2*. Oxford: Ostprey Publishing.

Fremont-Barnes, G.; Fisher, T. (2004)a: *The Napoleonic Wars: The Rise and Fall of an Empire*. Oxford: Osprey Publishing.

Fremont-Barnes, G. (2004)b: *The Napoleonic Wars: Peninsular War 1807-1814 v. 3*. Oxford: Osprey Publishing.

Fremont-Barnes, G. (2004)c: *The Napoleonic Wars: Fall of French Imperium 1813-1815 v. 4*. Oxford: Osprey Publishing.

Gates, D. (1997): *The Napoleonic Wars 1803-1815*. London: A Hodder Arnold Publication.

Hirshleifer, J. (2001): *The Dark Side of the Force*. Cambridge: Cambridge University Press.

Hofschröer, P. (2001): *Lützen & Bautzen 1813*. Oxford: Osprey Publishing.

Lanchester, F.W. (1916), *Aircraft in Warfare: The dawn of the fourth arm*. Constable. (1956) Extract reprinted in James R. Newmann (Ed.), *The World of mathematics* 4: 2138 2157. New York: Simon & Schuster.

Marshall, A. (1977). Principles of Economics: an introductory text. London: Macmillan.

Muir, R. (1998): *Tactics and the Experience of Battle in the Age of Napoleon*. New Haven: Yale University Press.

Nowak, H. u.a. (1996): *Lexikon zur Schlacht bei Jena und Auerstedt 1806*. Jena: Städtische Museen Jena.

Rothenberg, G. (2000): *Die Napoleonischen Kriege*. Berlin: Brandenburgisches Verlagshaus.

Schelling, TC. (1960): *The Strategy of Conflict*. Cambridge: Harvard University Press.

Smith, D. (1998): *The Greenhill Napoleonic Wars Data Book*. London: Greenhill Books.

Smith, D. (2005): *The Decline and Fall of Napleon's Empire*. London: Greenhill Books.

Sydsaeter, K.; Hammond, P. (2008): *Essential Mathematics for Economic Analysis*. New York:Prentice Hall.

Thiele, R. (1996): *Jena und Auerstedt 1806*. Frankfurt/Main: Report-Verlag.

Tullock, G. (1980). Efficient rent seeking. In: Buchanan, J.M.; Tollison, R.D.; Tullock, G. (eds). *Towards a theory of the rent-seeking society*. College Station: Texas A&M University Press.

Tullock, G. (2005): *The social dilemma: The economics of war and revolution*. Indianapolis, Ind.: University Publications.

Tutz, G. (2000): *Die Analyse kategorialer Daten*. München and Oldenbourg: Oldenbourg Wissensch. Vlg.

Uffindel, A. (2003): *Great Generals of the Napoleonic War and Their Battles*. Spellmount Publishers Ltd.

Wenzlik, D. (2001): *Marschall Macdonald: Herzog von Tarent*. Hamburg: VRZ Verlag GmbH.

Wenzlik, D. (2002)a: *Napoleon im Land der Pyramiden*. Hamburg: VRZ Verlag GmbH.

Wenzlik, D. (2002)b: *Unter der Fahne des Schwarzen Herzogs 1809*. Hamburg: VRZ Verlag GmbH.

Wenzlik, D. (2004)a: *Die Schlacht von Albuera*. Hamburg: VRZ Verlag GmbH.

Wenzlik, D. (2004)b: *Die Schlacht von Coruna*. Hamburg: VRZ Verlag GmbH.

Wenzlik, D. (2004)c: *Die Schlachten bei Oporto und Talevera*. Hamburg: VRZ Verlag GmbH.

Wenzlik, D.; Handrick, W. (2006): *Die Schlacht bei Auerstedt*. Hamburg: VRZ Verlag GmbH.

Wenzlik, D. (2008)a: *Waterloo I: Der Feldzug von 1815*. Hamburg: VRZ Verlag GmbH.

Wenzlik, D. (2008)b: *Waterloo II: Der Feldzug von 1815*. Hamburg: VRZ Verlag GmbH.

Wenzlik, D. (2008)c: *Waterloo III: Der Feldzug von 1815*. Hamburg: VRZ Verlag GmbH.

Wooldridge, J.M. (2005): *Indroductory Econometrics: A Modern Approach*. Stamford: Thomson Learning.

Papers

Brackney, H. (1956). The Dynamics of Military Combat. *Operations Research* 7(1): 30 – 44.

Dixit, A. (1987). Strategic behavior in contests. *American Economic Review* 77: 891 – 898.

Hirshleifer, J. (1989). Conflict and rent-seeking success functions: Ratio vs. difference models of relative success. *Public Choice* 63: 101 – 120.

Krueger, A. (1974). The Political Economy of the Rent-Seeking Society. *American Economic Review* 64(3): 291 – 303.

Michaels, R. (1988). The design of rent-seeking competitions. *Public Choice* 56: 17 – 29.

Skaperdas, S. (1994). Contest success functions. *Economic Theory* 7: 283 – 290.

Tullock, G. (1967). The Welfare Costs of Tariffs, Monopolies and Theft. *Western Economic Journal* 5(3): 224 – 232.

Willard, D. (1962). Lanchester as Force in History: An Analysis of Land Battles of the Years 1618 – 1905. *Research Analysis Corporation* RAC-TP-74: November 1962.

Appendix

Appendix A

We want to prove that for every Ratio Contest Success Function there exists a Difference Contest Success Function that has the same increase at a combination where all the contestants put the same effort into the contest. For a battle the case with two players is relevant. We then can express both functions easily:

$$p_1^{RCSF} = \frac{c_1^m}{c_1^m + c_2^m}$$

$$p_1^{DCSF} = \frac{e^{\gamma c_1}}{e^{\gamma c_1} + e^{\gamma c_2}}$$

The probability increase at a certain point of effort is determined by the first order derivate of the function. We now will calculate these.

$$\frac{\partial p_1^{RCSF}}{\partial c_1} = \frac{m \cdot c_1^{m-1} \cdot c_2^m}{(c_1^m \cdot c_2^m)^2}$$

$$\frac{\partial p_1^{DCSF}}{\partial c_1} = \frac{\gamma \cdot e^{\gamma c_1} \cdot e^{\gamma c_2}}{(e^{\gamma c_1} + e^{\gamma c_2})^2}$$

All the contestants now employ the same effort, so that all do have the same chance of winning the contest. Therefore c_1 and c_2 are the same and we can rephrase our derivates:

$$\frac{\partial p_1^{RCSF, c_1 = c_2}}{\partial c} = \frac{m}{4c}$$

$$\frac{\partial p_1^{DCSF, c_1 = c_2}}{\partial c} = \frac{\gamma}{4}$$

We want to calculate the values for m and γ given a certain $c_1 = c_2$, so that the increases are the same. So both derivates need to be equal.

$$\frac{\partial p_1^{RCSF, c_1 = c_2}}{\partial c} = \frac{\partial p_1^{DCSF, c_1 = c_2}}{\partial c}$$

$$\rightarrow \frac{m}{4c} = \frac{\gamma}{4} \qquad \text{q.e.d.}$$

$$\rightarrow \frac{m}{c} = \gamma$$

Whenever $m = \gamma \cdot c$ holds true, the increases of both CSF will be the same at the point where $c_1 = c_2$.

Appendix B

The following five pages are the data set used to obtain the empirical results for this analysis. Although most of the data is self explanatory, one variable needs further elucidation: AC is an alpha code used to show where the fights took place. Every combination of two letters is a code for the region of the battle.

AD	Adriatic	IM	Central Italy
CH	Switzerland	IN	Northern Italy
DK	Denmark	IS	Southern Italy
DV	Danube Valley	MD	Mediterranean
EC	Central Spain	MR	Middle Rhine
EE	Eastern Spain	NL	Netherlands
EG	Northwestern Spain	OP	East Prussia
EM	Spain, Madrid Area	PN	Northern Portugal
EN	Northern Spain	PM	Central Portugal
EW	Western Spain	PS	Southern Portugal
FC	France, Champagne	RM	Russia, main body
FE	Eastern France	RN	Russia, north flank guard
FJ	France, Jura Region	RS	Russia, south flank guard
FN	Northern France	RL	Russia, Latvia
FP	Pyrenees	SX	Saxony
FS	Southern France	TY	Tyrol
FW	Western France	UR	Upper Rhine
GB	Great Britain	WW	Warsaw
GN	Northern Germany	YE	Egypt

	AC	Day	Month	Year	Nap	Fr	ForFr	LosFr	VFr	Br	Pr	Aus	Rus	SP	UN	ForCo	LosCo	VCo
1	DV	20	4	1809	1	1	20500	479	1	0	0	1	0	0	0	22000	9800	0
2	PM	16	5	1811	0	1	23000	7000	0	1	0	0	0	1	0	35284	5904	1
3	EE	23	5	1809	0	1	8455	800	0	0	0	0	0	1	0	8546	300	1
4	YE	21	3	1801	0	1	10000	3500	0	1	0	0	0	0	0	12000	1529	1
5	EM	11	8	1809	0	1	18200	2400	1	0	0	0	0	1	0	23000	5300	0
6	XX	20	11	1793	0	1	25000	8000	0	0	0	0	0	0	1	20000	2000	1
7	FN	20	3	1814	1	1	30000	4200	0	0	0	1	1	0	0	43000	3000	1
8	IN	15	11	1796	1	1	20000	3500	1	0	0	1	0	0	0	18500	6200	0
9	DV	21	5	1809	1	1	65000	23000	0	0	0	1	0	0	0	98249	19690	1
10	OP	14	10	1806	0	1	29963	7000	1	0	1	0	0	0	0	51800	13000	0
11	DV	2	12	1805	1	1	65000	10500	1	0	0	1	1	0	0	86025	36000	0
12	ES	19	7	1808	0	1	22000	3000	0	0	0	0	0	1	0	17103	1000	1
13	FE	26	2	1814	0	1	30000	3100	0	0	0	1	1	0	0	30000	1900	1
14	ES	5	3	1811	0	1	10700	2562	0	1	0	0	0	1	0	8217	1238	1
15	IN	8	9	1796	1	1	20000	400	1	0	0	1	0	0	0	11000	2600	0
17	SX	20	5	1813	1	1	167000	22000	1	0	1	0	1	0	0	97000	11000	0
18	EN	9	12	1813	0	1	65933	5914	0	1	0	0	0	1	0	69000	4650	1
20	RM	26	11	1812	0	1	7000	0	1	0	0	0	1	0	0	5000	0	1
21	NL	19	9	1799	0	1	22000	3000	1	1	0	0	1	0	0	23000	4475	0
22	UR	2	10	1796	0	1	35000	500	1	0	0	1	0	0	0	15000	4300	0
23	EN	31	8	1813	0	1	34100	3801	0	1	0	0	0	1	0	22400	2406	1
24	RM	7	9	1812	1	1	103000	28000	1	0	0	0	1	0	0	120000	44000	0
25	FP	30	4	1794	0	1	30000	20	1	0	0	0	0	1	0	20000	3500	0
27	FN	29	1	1814	1	1	36000	3500	1	0	1	0	1	0	0	28000	3000	0
28	PM	27	9	1810	0	1	45774	4479	0	1	0	0	0	1	0	35765	1252	1
29	NL	7	8	1793	0	1	25435	200	0	1	0	1	0	0	0	43000	200	1
30	IN	12	11	1796	1	1	24000	1800	0	0	0	1	0	0	0	12000	1300	1
31	IN	29	10	1805	0	1	46000	8000	1	0	0	1	0	0	0	49000	5700	1
32	FP	17	11	1794	0	1	35000	3000	1	0	0	0	0	1	0	50000	10000	0
33	IS	9	3	1806	0	1	6000	200	1	0	0	0	0	0	1	10000	3000	0
34	EN	16	12	1808	0	1	15000	600	1	0	0	0	0	1	0	5000	2500	0
35	IN	20	6	1799	0	1	14000	1000	1	0	0	1	0	0	0	8000	2300	0

	AC	Day	Month	Year	Nap	Fr	ForFr	LosFr	VFr	Br	Pr	Aus	Rus	SP	UN	ForCo	LosCo	VCo
36	EE	13	4	1813	0	1	9600	1300	0	1	0	0	0	1	0	18200	400	1
37	IN	9	6	1800	1	1	12000	600	1	0	0	1	0	0	0	11000	4275	0
38	IN	5	8	1796	1	1	35000	1100	1	0	0	1	0	0	0	15500	3000	0
39	NL	6	10	1799	0	1	24000	1384	1	1	0	0	1	0	0	32000	2557	0
40	NL	26	4	1794	0	1	40000	7000	0	1	0	1	0	0	0	23000	2500	1
41	NL	3	6	1795	0	1	27000	2000	0	0	0	1	0	0	1	28000	424	1
42	XX	17	10	1793	0	1	25000	4000	1	0	0	0	0	0	1	40000	8000	0
43	EG	16	1	1809	0	1	20000	1563	0	1	0	0	0	0	0	14900	634	1
44	FN	7	3	1814	1	1	23000	6000	0	0	0	0	1	0	0	23000	4785	1
45	SX	6	9	1813	0	1	45000	20000	0	0	1	0	0	0	0	41000	6169	1
46	SX	26	8	1813	1	1	155000	10000	1	0	1	1	1	0	0	200000	23000	0
47	DV	22	4	1809	1	1	53000	3697	1	0	0	1	0	0	0	54000	7266	0
48	NL	2	10	1799	0	1	20000	3000	0	1	0	0	1	0	0	30000	1967	1
49	UR	19	10	1796	0	1	32000	2800	0	0	0	1	0	0	0	10000	1000	1
50	UR	3	5	1800	0	1	84000	3000	1	0	0	1	0	0	0	72000	1115	0
51	XX	27	10	1793	0	1	25000	4000	0	0	0	0	0	0	1	31000	2100	1
52	NL	23	5	1793	0	1	27000	3300	0	0	0	1	0	0	0	53000	1100	1
53	FN	25	3	1814	0	1	21000	6000	0	0	1	1	1	0	0	28000	2000	1
54	NL	16	6	1794	0	1	73000	3000	0	0	0	1	0	0	1	41000	3000	1
55	NL	26	6	1794	0	1	75000	5000	1	0	0	1	0	0	1	46000	1586	1
56	XX	25	5	1793	0	1	14000	4000	0	0	0	0	0	0	1	35000	1000	1
57	OP	14	6	1807	1	1	83321	12037	1	0	0	0	1	0	0	46000	15000	0
58	PM	3	5	1811	0	1	48452	2844	0	1	0	0	0	1	0	36946	1800	1
59	IN	4	11	1799	0	1	15000	7600	0	0	0	1	0	0	0	29000	2400	1
61	SX	2	5	1813	1	1	78000	19655	1	0	1	0	1	0	0	70000	12000	0
62	SX	30	10	1813	1	1	60000	10000	1	0	0	1	0	0	1	30000	6313	0
63	OP	10	6	1807	1	1	65000	12321	0	0	1	0	1	0	0	53000	5500	1
64	YE	20	3	1800	0	1	12000	600	1	0	0	0	0	0	1	40000	8000	0
65	UR	3	12	1800	0	1	76407	2500	1	0	0	1	0	0	1	58221	11595	0
66	NL	6	9	1793	0	1	42600	3000	1	0	0	1	0	0	1	17500	6000	0
67	NL	6	11	1792	0	1	43000	1950	1	0	0	1	0	0	0	13796	1241	0
68	OP	14	10	1806	1	1	54000	6794	1	0	1	0	0	0	1	47500	35000	0

	AC	Day	Month	Year	Nap	Fr	ForFr	LosFr	VFr	Br	Pr	Aus	Rus	SP	UN	ForCo	LosCo	VCo
69	UR	28	11	1793	0	1	34161	3100	0	0	1	0	0	0	0	26000	806	1
70	UR	23	5	1794	0	1	5000	1000	0	0	1	0	0	0	1	46000	110	1
71	SX	26	8	1813	0	1	35000	30000	0	0	1	0	1	0	0	86000	4000	1
73	SX	29	8	1813	0	1	37000	15000	0	0	1	1	1	0	0	70000	12319	1
75	XX	13	12	1793	0	1	25000	2000	1	0	0	0	0	0	1	25000	15000	0
76	SX	16	10	1813	1	1	203133	84112	0	0	1	1	1	0	0	361942	53774	1
77	NL	16	6	1815	1	1	60800	12000	1	0	1	0	0	0	0	86569	20000	0
78	IN	23	11	1795	0	1	25000	3000	1	0	0	1	0	0	1	18000	7000	0
79	IN	2	8	1796	1	1	20000	2000	1	0	0	1	0	0	0	15000	3000	0
80	XX	14	8	1793	0	1	10000	500	1	0	0	0	0	0	1	35000	5000	0
83	IN	5	4	1799	0	1	40600	8000	0	0	0	1	0	0	0	46000	6000	1
84	IS	4	7	1806	0	1	6440	2082	0	1	0	0	0	0	1	5060	327	1
85	MR	29	10	1795	0	1	33000	4800	0	0	0	1	0	0	1	27000	1600	1
86	RM	24	10	1812	1	1	24000	6000	0	0	0	0	1	0	0	24000	8000	1
87	UR	9	7	1796	0	1	36000	2400	1	0	0	1	0	0	0	32000	2600	0
88	IN	16	1	1797	1	1	28000	2000	1	0	0	1	0	0	0	4000	4000	0
89	IN	14	6	1800	1	1	28127	5600	1	0	0	1	0	0	0	28496	9402	0
90	EE	15	6	1809	0	1	10800	800	1	0	0	0	0	1	0	15000	5000	0
91	EW	29	3	1809	0	1	17000	700	1	0	0	0	0	1	0	24000	12000	0
92	EW	14	7	1808	0	1	13700	800	1	0	0	0	0	1	0	21350	3250	0
93	IN	25	12	1800	0	1	66000	4000	1	0	0	1	0	0	0	50000	8589	0
94	IN	8	2	1814	0	1	34000	3500	1	0	0	1	0	0	0	32000	4000	0
95	EN	21	12	1808	0	1	18000	400	1	0	0	0	0	1	0	7600	2200	0
96	FE	18	2	1814	1	1	30000	2000	2	0	0	1	0	0	1	15000	4000	0
97	FN	11	2	1814	1	1	25000	2100	1	0	1	0	1	0	0	32000	3387	0
98	UR	5	5	1800	0	1	52000	3000	1	0	0	1	0	0	0	48000	4000	0
99	YU	16	5	1809	0	1	13000	100	1	0	0	1	0	0	0	9000	1000	0
100	XX	29	6	1796	0	1	12000	2000	1	0	0	0	0	0	1	38000	5000	0
101	NL	18	3	1793	0	1	42500	5000	1	0	0	1	0	0	0	43000	2859	0
102	UR	11	8	1796	0	1	50000	2400	1	0	0	1	0	0	0	20000	2400	0
103	EN	10	11	1813	0	1	56650	4321	0	1	0	0	0	1	0	88000	2383	1
104	IN	15	8	1799	0	1	35000	11500	0	0	0	1	1	0	0	35000	6500	1

	AC	Day	Month	Year	Nap	Fr	ForFr	LosFr	VFr	Br	Pr	Aus	Rus	SP	UN	ForCo	LosCo	VCo
105	EM	18	11	1809	0	1	29000	1990	1	0	0	0	0	1	0	56439	18000	0
106	PN	29	3	1809	0	1	17000	2000	1	0	0	0	0	1	0	24000	8225	0
107	PN	12	5	1809	0	1	11200	2100	0	1	0	0	0	1	0	24000	48	1
109	FP	27	2	1814	0	1	34993	3985	0	1	0	0	0	1	0	44402	1645	1
110	FN	30	3	1814	0	1	41000	5000	0	0	1	1	1	0	1	58100	6705	1
111	IN	7	5	1809	0	1	44800	2000	1	0	0	1	0	0	0	20750	2894	0
112	RN	16	8	1812	0	1	18000	6000	1	0	0	0	1	0	0	22000	5500	1
113	RN	18	10	1812	0	1	23000	8500	1	0	0	0	1	0	0	40000	8000	1
115	OP	7	2	1807	1	1	75000	7600	1	0	1	0	1	0	0	63584	21800	0
116	OP	26	12	1806	0	1	26000	3900	1	0	0	0	1	0	0	40600	3500	1
118	NL	16	6	1815	0	1	26695	4400	1	0	0	0	0	0	1	30000	5000	1
119	IN	14	6	1809	0	1	35000	4018	1	0	0	1	0	0	0	31979	6235	0
121	PM	19	2	1811	0	1	7000	403	1	0	0	0	0	1	0	16030	4850	0
122	IN	14	1	1797	1	1	22000	3200	1	0	0	1	0	0	0	28000	12000	0
123	FN	1	2	1814	1	1	45000	5600	0	0	1	0	1	0	1	80000	6500	1
125	IN	16	4	1809	0	1	37050	6500	0	0	0	1	0	0	0	39000	3149	1
126	EW	22	7	1812	0	1	49652	24000	0	1	0	0	0	1	0	51939	4762	1
127	UR	24	10	1796	0	1	32000	1200	0	0	0	1	0	0	0	24000	800	1
129	RM	17	8	1812	1	1	50000	8564	1	0	0	0	1	0	0	30000	6000	1
130	EN	28	7	1813	0	1	30000	4000	0	1	0	0	0	1	0	24000	2600	1
131	UR	25	3	1799	0	1	38000	4000	1	0	0	1	0	0	0	46000	5800	0
132	EW	27	7	1809	0	1	46735	7268	0	1	0	0	0	0	0	55369	5608	1
133	EW	18	10	1809	0	1	11000	1377	0	0	0	0	0	1	0	21400	713	1
135	IC	3	5	1815	0	1	36009	4100	0	0	0	1	0	0	0	10733	810	1
136	FP	10	4	1814	0	1	42043	3236	0	1	0	0	0	1	0	49146	4558	1
137	NL	17	5	1794	0	1	82000	3000	1	0	0	1	0	0	1	48000	5500	0
138	NL	22	5	1794	0	1	45000	5950	0	0	0	1	0	0	1	28000	3000	1
139	IN	17	6	1799	0	1	33000	16500	0	0	0	1	1	0	0	37000	4059	1
140	FP	22	9	1793	0	1	22000	4500	0	0	0	0	0	1	0	17000	2000	1
141	EN	23	11	1808	0	1	31000	657	1	0	0	0	0	1	0	19000	4200	0
142	EM	13	1	1809	0	1	15500	200	1	0	0	0	0	1	0	12354	7323	0
143	EE	25	2	1809	0	1	13000	1000	1	0	0	0	0	1	0	13480	3000	0

	AC	Day	Month	Year	Nap	Fr	ForFr	LosFr	VFr	Br	Pr	Aus	Rus	SP	UN	ForCo	LosCo	VCo
144	RM	19	8	1812	0	1	41000	9000	1	0	0	0	1	0	0	22000	5000	1
145	IN	27	4	1799	0	1	28000	7500	0	0	0	1	1	0	0	24500	2000	1
146	PM	21	8	1808	0	1	16622	1800	0	1	0	0	0	1	0	18669	719	1
147	EN	21	6	1813	0	1	57300	8008	0	1	0	0	0	1	0	88276	4927	1
148	DV	5	7	1809	0	1	154100	30000	1	0	0	1	0	0	0	28468	41750	0
149	NL	18	6	1815	1	1	72000	42000	0	1	1	0	0	0	1	105950	22673	1
150	NL	15	10	1793	0	1	60000	5000	1	0	0	1	0	0	0	30000	3000	0
151	RM	18	10	1812	0	1	18000	3500	0	0	0	0	1	0	0	36000	1500	1
152	MR	3	9	1796	0	1	30000	3000	0	0	0	1	0	0	0	17000	1500	1
153	DV	10	7	1809	0	1	30000	6000	1	0	0	1	0	0	0	46000	6000	1
154	CH	4	6	1799	0	1	45000	1600	0	0	0	1	0	0	0	53000	4400	1
155	CH	25	9	1799	0	1	33500	4000	1	0	0	0	1	0	0	19605	7000	0
156	RM	27	11	1812	0	1	12000	11500	0	0	0	0	1	0	0	12000	0	1
157	RM	28	11	1812	0	1	5300	3000	0	0	0	0	1	0	0	8000	0	1
158	RM	28	11	1812	0	1	7000	5000	0	0	0	0	1	0	0	12000	2600	1

Appendix C

We start by considering the Ratio CSF for two players as mentioned in chapter 7.

$$p_{Fr} = \frac{(kc_{Fr})^m}{(kc_{Fr})^m + (c_{Co})^m}$$

As we do know nothing about k at the start we do not include it into the first regression we are running. We therefore estimate the following equation with the intercept being dropped:

$$(1) \qquad p_{Fr} = \beta_1 \frac{(c_{Fr})^m}{(c_{Fr})^m + (c_{Co})^m} + u.$$

β_1 can be interpreted to be a rough estimate for k^m, at least we expect $\beta_1 > 1$ for all $k^m > 1$ and $\beta_1 < 1$ for all $k^m < 1$. So β_1 is a pointer into the correct direction for the dimension of k^m. We now include β_1 into the formula by amending the part under the fraction bar:

$$(2) \qquad p_{Fr} = \beta_2 \frac{(c_{Fr})^m}{\beta_1 (c_{Fr})^m + (c_{Co})^m} + u.$$

We now obtain a β_2 that we expect to be nearer to k^m than before. By repeating these steps it is possible to estimate k^m, as we have found k^m when $\beta_i = \beta_{i-1} + \varepsilon$, where ε is the accuracy parameter specified by us. Hence it is possible to estimate k^m by a mixture of numerical and empirical tools.

Appendix D

```
> source("/Users/flotzin/Desktop/R/regressions.r")
> rcsf.search(0,3,5)
[1] "Best fit at: "
[1] 0.92
[1] 0.3909774
[1] "Best R2  at: "
[1] 0.83
[1] 0.5221564
> summary(rcsf(1,10))

Call:
lm(formula = VFr ~ 0 + I(Frm/ForAllm))

Residuals:
    Min      1Q  Median      3Q     Max
-0.7685 -0.4688  0.1262  0.4801  0.7796

Coefficients:
               Estimate Std. Error t value Pr(>|t|)
I(Frm/ForAllm)  0.98956    0.08191   12.08   <2e-16 ***
---
Signif. codes:  0 '***' 0.001 '**' 0.01 '*' 0.05 '.' 0.1 ' ' 1

Residual standard error: 0.491 on 132 degrees of freedom
Multiple R-squared: 0.5251, Adjusted R-squared: 0.5215
F-statistic: 145.9 on 1 and 132 DF,  p-value: < 2.2e-16

>
```

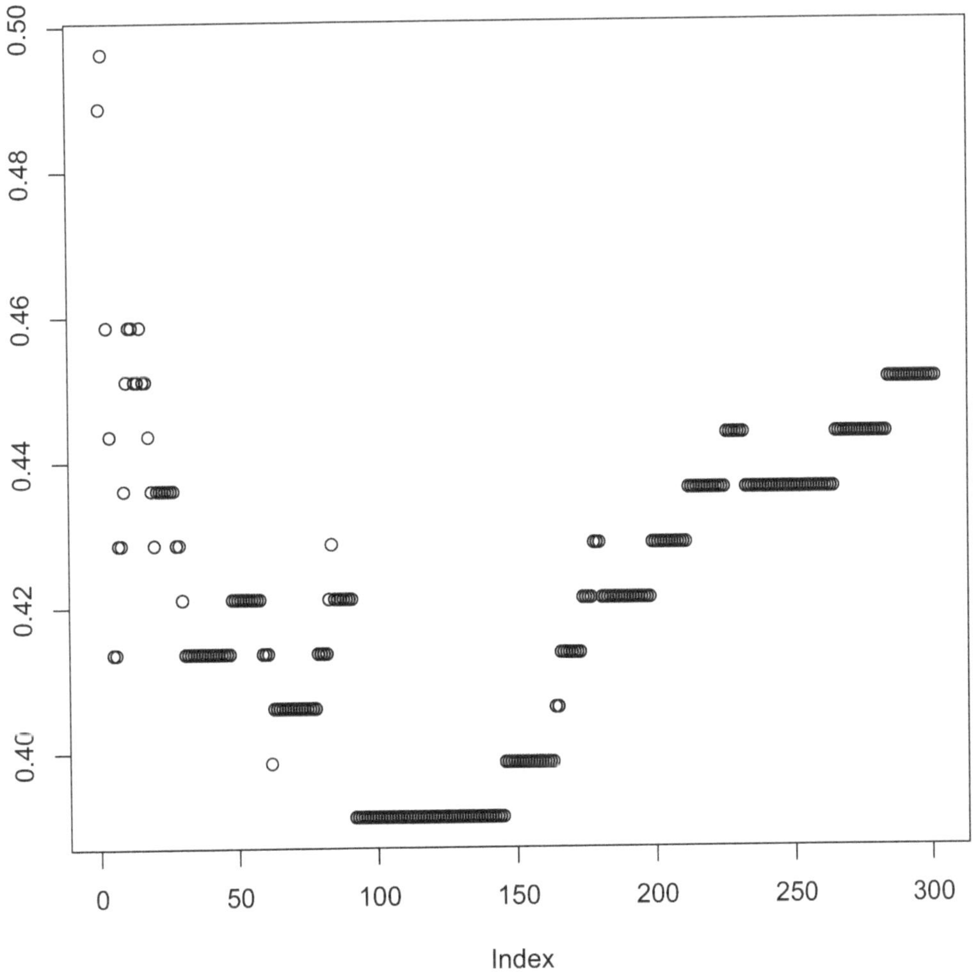
0.50
0.48
0.46
0.44
0.42
0.40
0
50
100
150
200
250
300
Index

```
> source("/Users/flotzin/Desktop/R/regressions.r")
> rcsf.search(0,3,5)
[1] "Best fit at: "
[1] 2.41
[1] 0.3082707
[1] "Best R2  at: "
[1] 0.76
[1] 0.5432029
> summary(rcsf(2.5,10))

Call:
lm(formula = VFr ~ 0 + I(Frm/ForAllm) + Nap)

Residuals:
    Min      1Q  Median      3Q     Max 
-1.0431 -0.2826 -0.0431  0.4800  0.9830 

Coefficients:
               Estimate Std. Error t value Pr(>|t|)    
I(Frm/ForAllm)  0.39528    0.04786   8.260 1.39e-13 ***
Nap             0.35627    0.09921   3.591 0.000464 ***
---
Signif. codes:  0 ‘***’ 0.001 ‘**’ 0.01 ‘*’ 0.05 ‘.’ 0.1 ‘ ’ 1

Residual standard error: 0.5033 on 131 degrees of freedom
Multiple R-squared: 0.5047, Adjusted R-squared: 0.4971
F-statistic: 66.74 on 2 and 131 DF,  p-value: < 2.2e-16

>
```

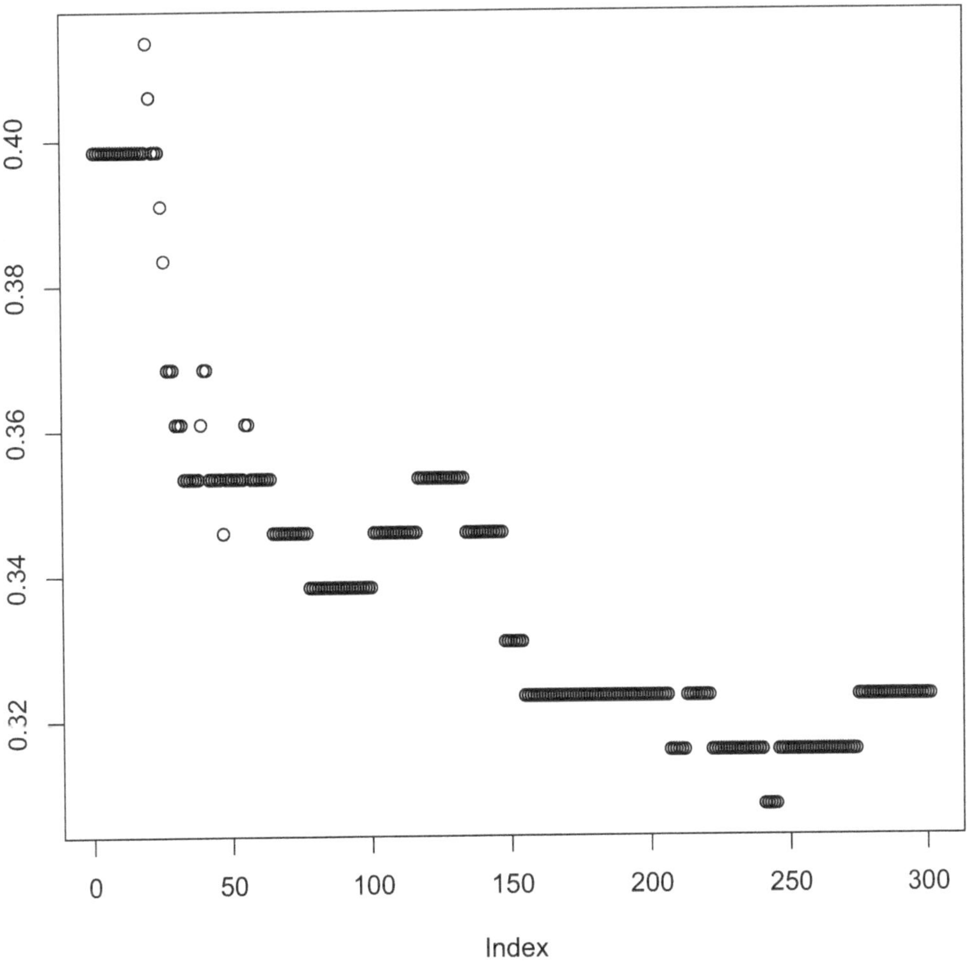
0.40
0.38
0.36
0.34
0.32
0
50
100
150
200
250
300
Index

```
> source("/Users/flotzin/Desktop/R/regressions.r")
> rcsf.search(0,3,5)
[1] "Best fit at: "
[1] 1.17
[1] 0.3007519
[1] "Best R2  at: "
[1] 0.69
[1] 0.5453524
> summary(rcsf(1.17,10))

Call:
lm(formula = VFr ~ 0 + I((1 - Nap) * Frm/ForAllm) + I(Nap * Frm/

Residuals:
     Min       1Q   Median       3Q      Max
-0.96277 -0.41071 -0.04998  0.46859  0.85986

Coefficients:
                           Estimate Std. Error t value Pr(>|t|)
I((1 - Nap) * Frm/ForAllm)  0.70587    0.07744   9.115 1.18e-15
I(Nap * Frm/ForAllm)        1.10764    0.12866   8.609 2.01e-14
---
Signif. codes:  0 '***' 0.001 '**' 0.01 '*' 0.05 '.' 0.1 ' ' 1

Residual standard error: 0.4822 on 131 degrees of freedom
Multiple R-squared: 0.5454, Adjusted R-squared: 0.5385
F-statistic:  78.6 on 2 and 131 DF,  p-value: < 2.2e-16

>
```

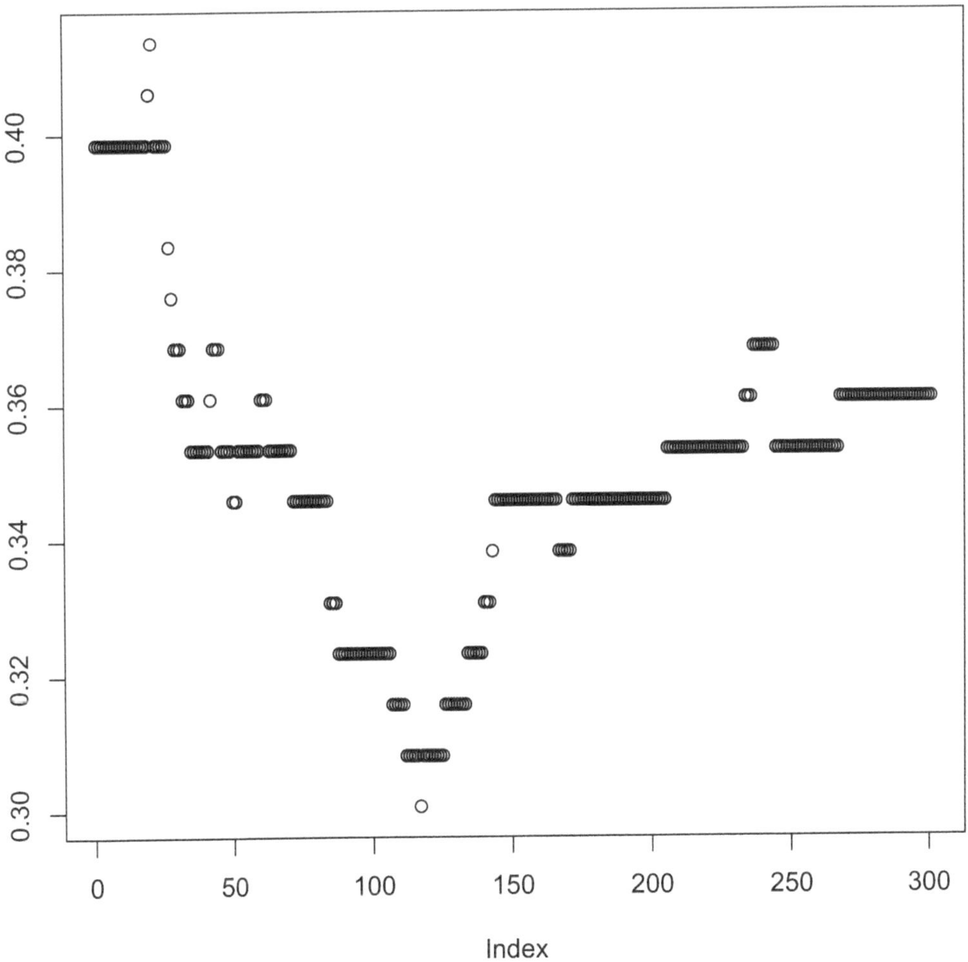

0.30
0.32
0.34
0.36
0.38
0.40
0
50
100
150
200
250
300
Index

```
> source("/Users/flotzin/Desktop/R/regressions.r")
> rcsf.search(0,3,5)
[1] "Best fit at: "
[1] 1.07
[1] 0.3233083
[1] "Best R2  at: "
[1] 0.59
[1] 0.5423498
> summary(rcsf(1.07,10))

Call:
lm(formula = VFr ~ 0 + I((1 - Nap) * Frm/ForAllm) + I(Nap * Frm/
    Nap)

Residuals:
     Min       1Q   Median       3Q      Max
-0.91184 -0.41658 -0.06298  0.43844  0.84101

Coefficients:
                           Estimate Std. Error t value Pr(>|t|)
I((1 - Nap) * Frm/ForAllm)  0.72234    0.07905   9.138 1.09e-15
I(Nap * Frm/ForAllm)        0.92237    0.50136   1.840   0.0681
Nap                         0.14242    0.32466   0.439   0.6616
---
Signif. codes:  0 '***' 0.001 '**' 0.01 '*' 0.05 '.' 0.1 ' ' 1

Residual standard error: 0.4824 on 130 degrees of freedom
Multiple R-squared: 0.5485, Adjusted R-squared: 0.5381
F-statistic: 52.64 on 3 and 130 DF,  p-value: < 2.2e-16

>
```

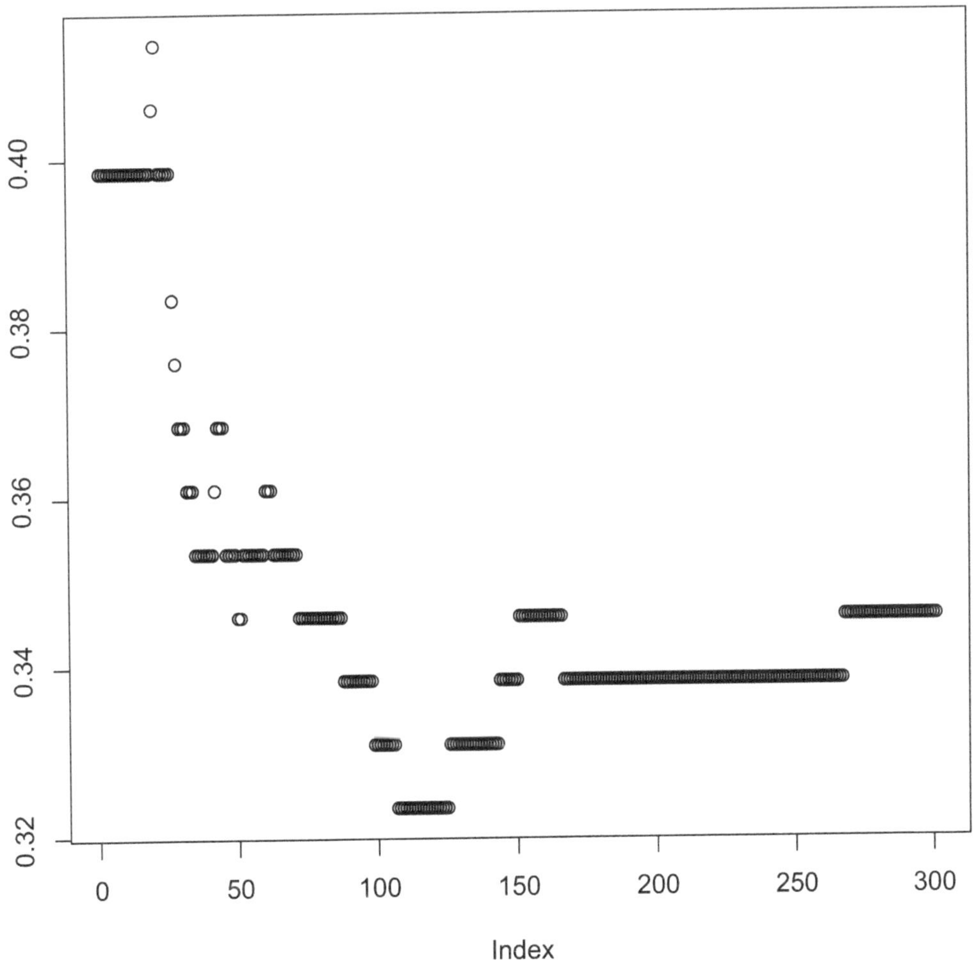
0.32
0.34
0.36
0.38
0.40
0
50
100
150
200
250
300
Index

Appendix E

Group of functions for easier access in R

- rcsf
- rcsf.search
- rcsf.fit
- rcsf.summary

```
# regression no 4
# -> to be started only after reg.R has been run as a startup script
# source("/Users/flotzin/Desktop/R/reg.R")

# question: Did Napoleon have any kind of impact on the troops commanded by him?
# question: Was Napoleon superior to the other generals of his time?
#

#-----------------------------------------------------------------------------------------


# start of own function "rcsf"
# <- ratio contest success function
# doing several iterations to approximate the effect parameters

rcsf <- function(m, iteration) {

  Frm <- ForFr^m
  mep <- 1

  while ( iteration >= 0 ) {
    ForAllm    <- ForCo^m + (ForFr^m)*mep
    iteration <- iteration - 1
#    func       <- lm(VFr ~ 0 + I( Frm / ForAllm) )
#    func       <- lm(VFr ~ 0 + I( Frm / ForAllm) + Nap )
    func       <- lm(VFr ~ 0 + I( (1- Nap) * Frm / ForAllm) + I(Nap * Frm / ForAllm) )
#    func       <- lm(VFr ~ 0 + I( (1- Nap) * Frm / ForAllm) + I(Nap * Frm / ForAllm) + Nap )
    mep        <- abs(func$coefficients[1])
  }

  rcsf     <- func

}


# start of own function "rcsf.summary"
# <- gives summary of rcsf

rcsf.summary <- function(m, iteration) {

    fit    <- rcsf.fit(m, iteration)
    print("Fit                  : ")
    print(fit)
    print("wrong results    : ")
    print(I(fit*lds))
    print("correct results : ")
    print(I((1-fit)*lds))

}


# start of own function "rcsf.fit"
# <- gives fit (wrong results / number of results) of rcsf

rcsf.fit <- function(m, iteration) {

    pred       <- predict.lm(rcsf(m, iteration))
    pred[which(pred<0.5)] <- 0 ; pred[which(pred>0.5)] <- 1
    forcast1   <- pred - VFr
    forcast1   <- abs(forcast1)
    rcsf.fit   <-  sum(forcast1) / ( lds )

}


# start of own function "rcsf.search"
# <- conducts a search for optimal mass effect parameter

rcsf.search <- function(m, endm, iteration) {

  mfittrack    <- {}
  mr2track     <- {}
```

```
  smallestfit <- 1
  highestr2   <- 0
  mcount     <<- {}
  fitcount   <<- {}
  r2count    <<- {}

  while ( m < endm ) {
    mcount    <<- c(mcount, m)
    m          <-  m + 0.01
    fit        <-  rcsf.fit(m, iteration)
    if( fit < smallestfit ) { mfittrack <- m; smallestfit <- fit }
    fitcount  <<- c(fitcount, fit)
    r.squared <-  summary(rcsf(m, iteration))$adj.r.squared
    if( r.squared > highestr2 ) { mr2track <- m; highestr2 <- r.squared }
    r2count   <<- c(r2count, r.squared)
  }

  print("Best fit at: ")
  print(mfittrack)
  print(smallestfit)
  print("Best R2  at: ")
  print(mr2track)
  print(highestr2)

}



# end of own function set "rcsf"
# <- ratio contest success function
```

Appendix F

R functions used to calculate Difference CSF

```
# regression no 1
# -> to be started only after reg.R has been run as a startup script

# logit regression


logit        <- glm(VFr ~ ForFr + Br + Pr + Rus + Aus + SP + UN), family=binomial(link="logit"))
#logit       <- glm(VFr ~ ForFr + Br + Pr + Rus + Aus + SP + UN + Nap,
                 family=binomial(link="logit"))
#logit       <- glm(VFr ~ I((1-Nap)*ForFr) + I(Nap*ForFr) + Br + Pr + Rus + Aus + SP + UN,
                 family=binomial(link="logit"))
#logit       <- glm(VFr ~ I((1-Nap)*ForFr) + I(Nap*ForFr) + Br + Pr + Rus + Aus + SP + UN + Nap,
                 family=binomial(link="logit"))

predlogit    <- predict.glm(logit)
predresponse <- predict.glm(logit, type="response")

pred <- predresponse
pred[which(pred<0.5)] <- 0 ; pred[which(pred>0.5)] <- 1
fit  <- pred - VFr
fit  <- abs(fit)
y    <- sum(fit)
x    <- sum(fit)
ch   <- (y - x) * 2
fit  <- sum(fit) / (length(pred) - ch)
coef <- cbind(exp(logit$coefficients[1:10]))
```

Appendix G

1 Summary of DCSF for Model 1
2 Summary of DCSF for Model 2
3 Summary of DCSF for Model 3
4 Summary of DCSF for Model 4
5 Summary of DCSF for Model 5

```
> source("/Users/flotzin/Desktop/R/regressions.r")
> summary(logit)

Call:
glm(formula = VFr ~ 0 + ForFr + Br + Pr + Rus + Aus + SP + UN,
    family = binomial(link = "logit"))

Deviance Residuals:
    Min       1Q   Median       3Q      Max
-1.9834  -1.1128   0.2177   0.9123   2.5594

Coefficients:
        Estimate Std. Error z value Pr(>|z|)
ForFr  3.822e-05  1.304e-05   2.931 0.003383 **
Br    -2.281e-04  6.105e-05  -3.736 0.000187 ***
Pr    -2.315e-05  1.571e-05  -1.474 0.140496
Rus   -3.153e-05  1.579e-05  -1.997 0.045818 *
Aus   -2.895e-05  1.512e-05  -1.915 0.055495 .
SP     1.762e-05  2.752e-05   0.640 0.522022
UN    -1.855e-05  2.029e-05  -0.914 0.360616
---
Signif. codes:  0 ‘***’ 0.001 ‘**’ 0.01 ‘*’ 0.05 ‘.’ 0.1 ‘ ’ 1

(Dispersion parameter for binomial family taken to be 1)

    Null deviance: 184.38  on 133  degrees of freedom
Residual deviance: 146.42  on 126  degrees of freedom
```

```
AIC: 160.42

Number of Fisher Scoring iterations: 6

> fit
[1] 0.2781955
> coef
           [,1]
ForFr 1.0000382
Br    0.9997719
Pr    0.9999768
Rus   0.9999685
Aus   0.9999711
SP    1.0000176
UN    0.9999815
<NA>         NA
<NA>         NA
<NA>         NA
>
```

```
> source("/Users/flotzin/Desktop/R/regressions.r")
> summary(logit)

Call:
glm(formula = VFr ~ 0 + ForFr + Br + Pr + Rus + Aus + SP + UN +
    Nap, family = binomial(link = "logit"))

Deviance Residuals:
    Min       1Q   Median       3Q      Max
-1.8832  -1.1016   0.2561   0.8200   2.5965

Coefficients:
        Estimate Std. Error z value Pr(>|z|)
ForFr  3.186e-05  1.367e-05   2.330 0.019799 *
Br    -2.186e-04  6.077e-05  -3.597 0.000321 ***
Pr    -2.571e-05  1.704e-05  -1.509 0.131379
Rus   -3.768e-05  1.691e-05  -2.228 0.025873 *
Aus   -2.769e-05  1.597e-05  -1.734 0.082879 .
SP     2.252e-05  2.791e-05   0.807 0.419675
UN    -1.627e-05  2.036e-05  -0.799 0.424165
Nap    1.155e+00  5.647e-01   2.045 0.040859 *
---
Signif. codes:  0 ‘***’ 0.001 ‘**’ 0.01 ‘*’ 0.05 ‘.’ 0.1 ‘ ’ 1

(Dispersion parameter for binomial family taken to be 1)

    Null deviance: 184.38  on 133  degrees of freedom
```

```
Residual deviance: 141.71  on 125  degrees of freedom
AIC: 157.71

Number of Fisher Scoring iterations: 6

> fit
[1] 0.2556391
> coef
           [,1]
ForFr 1.0000319
Br    0.9997814
Pr    0.9999743
Rus   0.9999623
Aus   0.9999723
SP    1.0000225
UN    0.9999837
Nap   3.1733375
<NA>         NA
<NA>         NA
>
```

```
> source("/Users/flotzin/Desktop/R/regressions.r")
> summary(logit)

Call:
glm(formula = VFr ~ 0 + I((1 - Nap) * ForFr) + I(Nap * ForFr) +
    Br + Pr + Rus + Aus + SP + UN, family = binomial(link = "logit"))

Deviance Residuals:
     Min        1Q    Median        3Q       Max
-2.04014  -0.98873   0.03988   0.86895   2.74105

Coefficients:
                      Estimate Std. Error z value Pr(>|z|)
I((1 - Nap) * ForFr)  3.365e-05  1.406e-05   2.393 0.016697 *
I(Nap * ForFr)        7.435e-05  2.132e-05   3.488 0.000487 ***
Br                   -2.194e-04  6.046e-05  -3.629 0.000285 ***
Pr                   -4.445e-05  1.922e-05  -2.313 0.020724 *
Rus                  -6.441e-05  2.173e-05  -2.964 0.003036 **
Aus                  -3.332e-05  1.688e-05  -1.974 0.048362 *
SP                    2.086e-05  2.790e-05   0.748 0.454610
UN                   -1.547e-05  2.066e-05  -0.749 0.454038
---
Signif. codes:  0 ‘***’ 0.001 ‘**’ 0.01 ‘*’ 0.05 ‘.’ 0.1 ‘ ’ 1

(Dispersion parameter for binomial family taken to be 1)

    Null deviance: 184.38  on 133  degrees of freedom
```

```
Residual deviance: 138.31  on 125  degrees of freedom
AIC: 154.31

Number of Fisher Scoring iterations: 6

> fit
[1] 0.2330827
> coef
                           [,1]
I((1 - Nap) * ForFr) 1.0000337
I(Nap * ForFr)       1.0000744
Br                   0.9997806
Pr                   0.9999556
Rus                  0.9999356
Aus                  0.9999667
SP                   1.0000209
UN                   0.9999845
<NA>                        NA
<NA>                        NA
>
```

```
> source("/Users/flotzin/Desktop/R/regressions.r")
> summary(logit)

Call:
glm(formula = VFr ~ 0 + I((1 - Nap) * ForFr) + I(Nap * ForFr) +
    Br + Pr + Rus + Aus + SP + UN + Nap, family = binomial(link = "logit"))

Deviance Residuals:
     Min        1Q    Median        3Q       Max
-2.03808  -0.99073   0.04407   0.86966   2.73548

Coefficients:
                       Estimate Std. Error z value Pr(>|z|)
I((1 - Nap) * ForFr)  3.330e-05  1.438e-05   2.315  0.02062 *
I(Nap * ForFr)        7.202e-05  2.866e-05   2.513  0.01198 *
Br                   -2.190e-04  6.056e-05  -3.615  0.00030 ***
Pr                   -4.361e-05  2.047e-05  -2.130  0.03316 *
Rus                  -6.333e-05  2.348e-05  -2.697  0.00699 **
Aus                  -3.292e-05  1.724e-05  -1.910  0.05618 .
SP                    2.115e-05  2.803e-05   0.755  0.45037
UN                   -1.537e-05  2.067e-05  -0.743  0.45729
Nap                   9.550e-02  7.970e-01   0.120  0.90462
---
Signif. codes:  0 '***' 0.001 '**' 0.01 '*' 0.05 '.' 0.1 ' ' 1

(Dispersion parameter for binomial family taken to be 1)
```

```
    Null deviance: 184.38  on 133  degrees of freedom
Residual deviance: 138.29  on 124  degrees of freedom
AIC: 156.29

Number of Fisher Scoring iterations: 6

> fit
[1] 0.2406015
> coef
                         [,1]
I((1 - Nap) * ForFr) 1.0000333
I(Nap * ForFr)       1.0000720
Br                   0.9997811
Pr                   0.9999564
Rus                  0.9999367
Aus                  0.9999671
SP                   1.0000212
UN                   0.9999846
Nap                  1.1002116
<NA>                        NA
>
```

```
> source("/Users/flotzin/Desktop/R/regressions.r")
> summary(logit)

Call:
glm(formula = VFr ~ 0 + I((1 - Nap) * ForFr) + I(Nap * ForFr) +
    Br + Pr + Rus + Aus, family = binomial(link = "logit"))

Deviance Residuals:
     Min        1Q    Median        3Q       Max
-2.02845  -0.97931   0.04089   0.92917   2.66239

Coefficients:
                      Estimate Std. Error z value Pr(>|z|)
I((1 - Nap) * ForFr)  3.352e-05  1.155e-05   2.903 0.003699 **
I(Nap * ForFr)        7.435e-05  1.981e-05   3.753 0.000174 ***
Br                   -2.055e-04  5.789e-05  -3.550 0.000386 ***
Pr                   -4.543e-05  1.899e-05  -2.392 0.016743 *
Rus                  -6.446e-05  2.103e-05  -3.065 0.002177 **
Aus                  -3.356e-05  1.482e-05  -2.265 0.023524 *
---
Signif. codes:  0 ‘***’ 0.001 ‘**’ 0.01 ‘*’ 0.05 ‘.’ 0.1 ‘ ’ 1

(Dispersion parameter for binomial family taken to be 1)

    Null deviance: 184.38  on 133  degrees of freedom
Residual deviance: 139.81  on 127  degrees of freedom
AIC: 151.81
```

```
Number of Fisher Scoring iterations: 6

> fit
[1] 0.2180451
> coef
                             [,1]
I((1 - Nap) * ForFr) 1.0000335
I(Nap * ForFr)       1.0000743
Br                   0.9997945
Pr                   0.9999546
Rus                  0.9999355
Aus                  0.9999664
<NA>                        NA
<NA>                        NA
<NA>                        NA
<NA>                        NA
>
```